THE NEW SYSTEM EXPLAINED

Barbara Meredith

D0301197

**A C E
BOOKS**

© 1993 Barbara Meredith
Published by Age Concern England
1268 London Road
London SW16 4ER

Editor Caroline Hartnell
Design Eugenie Dodd
Production Marion Peat
Copy preparation Vinnette Marshall
Typesetting Rosemary Burnard
Printed and bound in Great Britain by Bell & Bain Ltd, Glasgow

A catalogue record for this book is available from the British Library.

ISBN 0–86242–121–7

Contents

Foreword

Many of the institutions which affect our lives are undergoing change. These changes are often preceded by long periods during which those affected have a phrase or a date in their minds and know that something rather important will be happening. However, they do not know exactly why the changes are occurring or what their effect will be. The advent of the single European market has been one such situation. The community care reforms are another.

Somewhere around a quarter of the population will be affected directly by the community care changes, either as recipients of a service or because of involvement with service provision. When we include those people indirectly affected, it is a much larger proportion. If those who will be working under the new arrangements understand their nature and purpose, then the transition is more likely to be smoothly introduced.

In addition to structural reform, changed attitudes will also be important for those who work within the new system. New lines of communication and cooperation have to be developed and will be greatly tested in the early days of change. New methods of planning and deciding priorities have to be introduced with the maximum sensitivity. These are tasks which will tax the skills of many people.

The changes do not apply only to older people, but older people with care needs will be the largest group affected. It is therefore very appropriate that Age Concern England should publish *The Community Care Handbook*, which describes the new arrangements and reflects on some implications of the reforms. It is my belief that it will help all who have to try to make the new system work, and I am privileged to have been invited to write this foreword.

Professor Sir Michael Drury, OBE
Chairman, Age Concern England

Michael Drury has been in general practice for 38 years.
He was Professor of General Practice at Birmingham University
and President of the Royal College of General Practitioners.

About the author

Barbara Meredith has been at Age Concern England for five years. Her work as an Information and Policy Officer has focused on the community care changes, and on issues related to funding and provision of long-term care for older people.

As an adult education teacher, Barbara Meredith worked with adults returning to study, as well as teaching examination courses in welfare rights and social administration. Her interest in services for and policies about older people has been sustained through welfare rights work, and through involvement in research projects at the London School of Economics and at the Policy Studies Institute. She is the author of *A Selected Bibliography of Social Planning for the Elderly*, published by the Centre for Policy on Ageing; and co-author with Susan Tester of *Ill-informed? A study of information and support for elderly people in the inner city* (Policy Studies Institute), and with Jane Lewis of *Daughters Who Care* (Routledge).

Acknowledgements

I owe particular thanks to colleagues at Age Concern for their support and advice. They include David Bookbinder, Shelagh Doonan, David Moncrieff, Marion Peat, Sally West, Jane Whelan and Robin Versteeg. Chapters 3–7 owe much to colleagues from Age Concern's Fieldwork Department, with whom I have worked for over a year to develop material for Age Concern organisations and others on the community care changes. They are Bob Anderson, Michael Boyd, Jane Jones, Mary Rutherford and Richard Wood. Vinnette Marshall has had the complex task of word processing successive versions of the text. Evelyn McEwen from Age Concern and Sheila Stace of NCVO provided detailed and most helpful comments on the first draft of the manuscript. Caroline Hartnell has exercised tremendous skill in editing the complex text, always with sympathetic and tactful support.

The responsibility for factual accuracy and for opinions expressed in the book rests with me. All names used in examples are fictitious.

I have received invaluable insights about how the community care changes are developing from social services and Age Concern personnel in several counties and metropolitan boroughs. I am grateful for the time which they shared with me.

Personal experience also enriches my view of community care. Community care is part of all our lives. It would be impossible to write about it without being influenced by the experiences of relatives, friends and neighbours. I also owe much to the insights which I gain daily in providing information to older people and their families. Their experiences are the litmus test of the quality of community care.

Barbara Meredith
January 1993

Preface

Since joining Age Concern in 1987, I have been working on aspects of the community care changes. I therefore welcomed the opportunity to write a book explaining the changes to people who have not been privileged over the years to follow them in minute detail.

The changes are complex and far-reaching. Not everyone agrees with every part of them, but they are here to stay. It is important that everyone involved with community care understands how they work, and what some of their effects might be. The aim of this book is to make it all more understandable. Chapters 1–8 describe the history of community care and explain the current changes. Chapter 9 reflects on aspects of the changes and the 'ideals' of community care.

The examples in the book will be about older people, but the text will relate to most adults who need care.

This book describes the provisions of the White Paper, *Caring for People*, and Part III of the NHS and Community Care Act 1990 in England. In Wales, the provisions of Part III of the Act apply, but there are differences from England in how the changes will be carried out. Separate sections of the White Paper and the Act apply to Scotland and are not dealt with in this book, nor is the situation in Northern Ireland, which was covered by neither the Act nor the White Paper. The changes mainly involve local authority social services departments. (In Scotland, services are organised slightly differently. Social services are provided by social work departments, and some arrangements are different from those in England and Wales.)

Introduction

ANNIE – A CASE STUDY IN COMMUNITY CARE

When Annie broke her hip, her carefully balanced world seemed to fall apart. She had managed the problems of Parkinson's disease with help from her family and neighbours, and she could still tend the garden if she moved slowly. Grandchildren came to stay, and her son and daughter visited regularly. She baked for her neighbour, in exchange for help in the garden and with heavy chores.

All that changed one summer afternoon when she tripped over the garden hose. Three months later, she was home from hospital with a new hip, and a new routine. The home help came several times a week at first, then less. Meals-on-wheels was started, but the food was unappetising, and the person who delivered the meals simply dashed in and out – not even time to say hello. This made Annie feel uncomfortable, and she decided not to continue with the meals.

The physiotherapist helped her learn to walk again, and she gradually gained strength. She worked hard to regain confidence, but her family were worried about how she would continue to cope with the stairs and a house which was really too large.

Sheltered flats were being built nearby. Her family urged Annie to move there, so that she could be on one floor, with help if she needed it. But Annie didn't feel able to face the upheaval. She had good neighbours, and she didn't want to give up the garden, or the space in case the grandchildren came to stay.

The boy next door took her shopping every week – until he went away to college. His mother had gone to work full time, so she wasn't around so much either. In the second year after her fall, Annie stayed in all winter, not even sitting in the garden when the warmer weather came. She fell frequently, but the alarm promised by the Council had never been put in, and she worried about how she would get help if she needed it. Her son and daughter worried about not being able to help more, but both had families and full-time jobs.

Two years after her fall, Annie fell and lay for several hours unable to move. She said she couldn't go on with the fear of falling, and she quickly made arrangements to go into a nearby residential home. She didn't really need 'care' – so much as support. She was quite capable of cooking her own meals and doing most things for herself, but once she was in the home, she didn't really need to any more. She was lovingly cared for, but had little opportunity to do much for herself. Her spirits and her abilities gradually declined.

As her illness progressed, Annie grew increasingly afraid about what might happen to her. She began to fall more frequently, and the home's owners warned her that she might not be able to stay if she became too dependent. Two years after entering the home, Annie relapsed, becoming bedridden and confused. In her lucid moments, she told her daughter that she wished she didn't have to carry on. The last few weeks of her life were spent peacefully and securely in a geriatric hospital.

Annie was a user of 'community care'. Before and after her fall she was supported in many ways by her family and neighbours. After she had her new hip, she was helped by nurses, the home help, the physiotherapist, and by meals on wheels, although the hoped-for alarm never materialised.

It wasn't as if she needed all that much care; but it didn't seem to be put together so that she felt confident staying at home. Her family found it hard to persuade her to consider living in a more suitable home, and there wasn't anyone else who had the time to help her to make that decision. Once Annie was in the care home, it was as if the 'community' was far away, even though she was only half a mile from her former home.

This book is about community care. It is written for the many people who may be involved in helping to provide community care for people like Annie. It will describe:

- what community care is, and why it is so important;
- the kinds of people who may need community care;

- the people and the organisations which may be involved in providing community care;
- the changes taking place in the provision and funding of some community care services and how these will work.

According to the Government the aim of community care is to help people with care needs to live as independent a life as possible in their own homes for as long as this is reasonable and practical. Yet this is not an easy task. The story of Annie illustrates good and bad aspects of the way community care works in practice: how easy it is to be in too much of a hurry to stop and talk; how much neighbours and friends can help, yet how difficult it is to depend on them given that their circumstances may change and they may not be able to help any more; how hard it sometimes seems to organise little things which might make a big difference – like an alarm; and how difficult it is for people to plan how they will deal with their own frailty.

The community care changes aim to help people find appropriate care through careful assessment and clear statements about what support is available in each area of the country. They are meant to create a system which will protect the interests of users of services, and raise the quality of services. Whether these changes will succeed depends partly on the amount of money available to carry them out. But it also depends on the attitudes of all the people who will be involved. The changes are complex and not always easy to understand. Many people have only the vaguest idea of what is happening. Yet everyone who is working 'in the community' needs to have some understanding of how the whole system works.

Readers should be warned that this book describes a constantly changing scene. It aims to provide the essential background information which people will need if they are to understand the community care changes, but its subject matter is not set in stone. If it improves understanding, and stimulates further thought and reflection, it will have succeeded in its objectives.

1 What is Community Care?

'Community care' has no single meaning. Broadly it means helping people who need care and support to live with dignity and as much independence as possible 'in the community'. The 'community' is hard to define. It most often means ordinary homes – but for some people it includes special forms of housing, or residential or nursing homes.

New arrangements are being introduced for publicly provided social services. These are often referred to as the 'community care changes'. They were first described in a 1989 Government document called *Caring for People*. The NHS and Community Care Act 1990 made the necessary legal changes.

It is important not to equate these 'community care changes' with 'community care'. This tends to happen partly because people have taken to referring to them as 'implementing community care', even talking about April 1993 as 'when community care comes in'. As we show in Chapter 2, community care has been around for many years.

WHAT ARE THE COMMUNITY CARE CHANGES?

The changes introduce new procedures for arranging and paying for state-funded social care. They are described in Chapters 3–8. Broadly, the Government has stated that they aim to:

- make the best use of public money – to make sure that the services which are provided by local and health authorities are provided for those who need them most, and actually meet their needs;

- encourage authorities to set priorities – to decide how they will spend money if there is not enough to provide for everyone's needs;
- ensure that local authorities check on the quality of care which is being provided – through inspection units, complaints procedures, care management, setting service specifications and monitoring contracts for care;
- encourage local authorities to use other organisations to provide services – not just to provide them themselves.

Before looking at the background to the changes, this chapter looks at the varied nature of community care – at who may use it, and at the different service providers.

WHAT IS COMMUNITY CARE?

Community care is like a jigsaw puzzle. It is the combination of support and services for a person with care needs. These include provision which is largely outside the scope of this book, such as pensions, benefits and income; transport; housing; the opportunity to work; policies for essential services, such as fuel and telephones; recreation, education and leisure.

The meaning of community care will depend on each person's needs:

Fred Upton is 69. He has lived for 48 years in a large mental handicap hospital which is being closed. As part of the closure programme, Mr Upton has been taking part in training to help him learn to manage outside the hospital. He is going to live in a small group home with some of his friends from hospital. They are going to live 'in the community'.

Mrs Prashar is 72. She has no children, and no relatives nearby. She has had a stroke and walks with a frame. After a period of rehabilitation in hospital, she has returned home. She has a battery-operated wheelchair in which she goes to the local shops. A nurse comes in the morning to help her get dressed, a home help sees to the cleaning, and her neighbour calls in several times a day and last thing at night. Mrs Prashar is living 'in the community'. She is a user of 'community care'.

John and Iris O'Donnell live in a block of flats in the inner city. Mrs O'Donnell has never gone out very much, and has few friends. She is becoming increasingly confused. She forgets to wash herself, and can't cook any more. Mr O'Donnell is upset about this, but doesn't know what to do. He does the shopping and the cooking, but finds the personal care for his wife increasingly difficult and embarrassing. Mr and Mrs O'Donnell live 'in the community', but they do not appear to be benefiting from 'community care'.

Community care is part of our lives. It is the web of care and support provided for frail, sick or dependent people both by their families or other members of the community and by public or other services.

This means helping some people remain in their homes, or creating homelike places with appropriate support. In general, community care means a preference for home life over 'institutional care'. It means helping people to be 'integrated' with their local community, rather than being separate from it, perhaps in a large long-stay hospital. Where people do live with others – in what are called 'communal' settings or 'group homes' – there is a general preference for smaller homes, close to where people have always lived.

Where is 'home'?

While it is generally agreed that community care means helping people to live the life of their choice, given their particular illness or disabilities, and preferably in their own homes, defining 'home' is not a simple matter. People with different needs may find appropriate care in different places. Each of these will be 'home' to the person who lives there. Examples of these include:

— a hostel or group home, for people who have been discharged from a long-stay hospital – perhaps with a support worker living in, or calling in regularly;

— the family home for a child with learning disabilities, later followed by a move to independent living, or to a small group home;

— a specially adapted house or flat for someone with physical disabilities;

— a residential or nursing home;

— a hospital, if that is where the person lives and the care there is appropriate to that person's needs (it is fair to say that most definitions of 'the community' do not include hospitals, but there is no reason why someone who lives in a long-stay hospital should be excluded from 'the community');

— a 'sheltered' home, with support from a warden and perhaps some extra care services available;

— a family home, which provides 'foster' or 'family-based' care for one or more people.

Physically living 'in the community' does not necessarily mean a good quality of life. For some people, living on their own 'in the community' may mean that they have less care and fewer friends than they might have in a communal home.

One dilemma of community care is how to get the balance right between helping people remain in their homes and not forcing them to do so when it is not their wish, or it is no longer possible for them to have a good quality of life at home.

What does community care involve?

Most community care is provided by family, neighbours and friends, although many people do not have such support. The ideal is that this care should be backed up where necessary by services which are appropriate for the needs of the people being cared for *and* their carers.

Although such services are organised differently in each area, users of services have some universal needs, including:

Information
To enable them to find out what is available, and from whom.

Practical support
Equipment, or adaptations to their homes, to help cope with particular disabilities.

Domestic assistance
To help with the tasks of everyday life.

Emotional support
To help them come to terms with their particular problem.

Physical and/or nursing care
To help with their illness or disability.

Financial support
To maintain a reasonable quality of life, and help to compensate for the costs of disability and, for many people, the loss of or reduction in earnings.

Appropriate housing
A warm and affordable place to live.

Access to transport
The ability to take part in community life.

Access to recreation and leisure and work.

Appropriate provision in all these respects should contribute to a better *quality of life* for the person with community care needs. What is appropriate will depend not only on the person's needs, but also on his or her expectations and personal preferences.

WHO USES COMMUNITY CARE?

Ordinary people use community care. They are people who happen to have special needs which mean that they cannot cope in one way or another with their own care. They may be ill, have a physical disability, be unable to perform some everyday tasks – like bathing or cleaning – or have lived for too many years in the limited environment of an institution.

Such people are often referred to in terms of 'client groups'. This is a kind of shorthand which focuses on the particular characteristics of groups of people. There is, however, a danger in thinking about people as belonging to client groups: in general, people do not think of themselves as carrying such a label.

A 78-year-old woman in hospital, after a hip replacement: 'The doctor came round yesterday with a group of students. He stood at the door and said, "These are my geriatrics". But *I'm* not geriatric.'

For planners and providers of services, it can be easy to forget that service users are unique individuals, each with their own needs and their own hopes. This applies to 'residents' of care homes, 'clients' of home care services, or 'the blind', 'the deaf' or 'the homeless' – all different people who happen to share similar circumstances or places of care. This definitely does not make them all the same. In thinking about the community care changes we must constantly remind ourselves not to become so bogged down in *process* that we forget the people for whom the care is intended. Each part of the process should be based firmly on what users of different services want for themselves.

Yet in order to plan for services it is convenient, perhaps necessary, to think of service users in terms of client groups. Keeping the balance between planning for groups of people and helping individuals with particular and unique needs is a great challenge.

Another way of reminding ourselves that we are talking about *people* is to remember to use that word when we talk about the client groups. Thus we talk about 'elderly people' rather than 'the elderly'; or 'people with mental health problems', rather than 'the mentally ill'. There used to be a Minister for the Disabled. This title was recently changed to 'Minister for Disabled People'. This may seem rather trivial, but it is a recognition that groups with special needs are made up of individual people.

Adult client groups

There are a number of adult 'client groups'. (This book does not cover children, whose needs include education as well as other aspects of community care. The Children Act 1989 has introduced many changes relevant to provision for children and their protection.) Adult client groups include:

Elderly people

This term generally refers to people aged over 65 – or to people over pension age, which is currently 60 for women and 65 for men. The 'elderly client group' covers an age span of 40 or more years. In 1991 it was estimated that there were 8,838,000 people aged 65 and over in Britain, and more than 10 million over pension age.

Ageing is not a disease, and it does not automatically produce ill health. However, as we age we are more likely to experience chronic illnesses or conditions which can lead to a need for care. A survey of disability in Great Britain found that almost 70 per cent of disabled adults were aged 60 or over, and nearly half were aged 70 or over. Forty per cent of the most severely disabled adults were aged 80 or over, and it is estimated that there will be well over a million people aged over 85 by the year 2001. It is these people who are most likely to need community care – although such generalisations mask the fact that many younger elderly people need care, while many very elderly people need no care at all.

Some care for elderly people is called 'geriatric' care. This word is most often used in the health services to refer to people over a certain age – perhaps 75 or 80. Geriatrics is a medical specialty which focuses on improving the situation of elderly people with illnesses or disabilities, taking into account all the medical and social factors needed for their care. Elderly people themselves do not always like to be referred to as 'geriatrics', as we have seen.

People with physical disabilities

People with physical disabilities can be of any age, but older age groups include larger proportions of people with physical disabilities than younger age groups. Physical disabilities may develop gradually, as with arthritis or degenerative changes to the spine; or suddenly, as with a stroke. Some mental illnesses or handicaps also cause problems of physical disability: people with advanced Alzheimer's disease may, for instance, have problems walking.

People with mental health problems

There is a wide range of mental illnesses, which affect people of all ages. Some are readily treated with medication; others respond to counselling and various types of therapy. Some, such as Alzheimer's disease, are progressive diseases as a result of which the patient's condition will gradually deteriorate. One in five people over the age of 80 is thought to be likely to develop this condition. If the actual numbers of this age group are rising, then there will be an increase in the numbers of people with Alzheimer's disease.

Surveys show that something between 10 and 12 per cent of people aged over 65 suffer from depression, a condition which is not always properly diagnosed.

Sometimes there is special reference to a client group known as 'elderly mentally ill', or 'EMI'. Another group is referred to as ESMI – elderly severely mentally ill. 'Psychogeriatrics' refers to specialist care for elderly people with mental illness.

A significant number of mentally ill people live in long-stay hospitals. Most could be resettled if appropriate housing and community support were available.

People with learning disabilities

(Formerly referred to as mentally handicapped people, or people with mental handicap, and sometimes referred to as people with learning difficulties.) At one time mentally handicapped people were most often cared for in long-stay hospitals. Now, as children, they mainly live with their parents; as adults, they should be helped to live in supported settings.

Many people with learning disabilities are still trapped in long-stay institutions, where they were sent many years ago. At the same time, those in the community are living much longer than they once did. As their parents grow older, they become increasingly concerned to ensure that their children will be well cared for after they die or become too frail to continue caring for them.

In recent years, people with learning disabilities have been encouraged through advocacy schemes to have more of a say about how they would like to live (see p 72).

NORMALISATION

'Normalisation' is the word often used to describe the principles of care for people with learning disabilities (formerly called mental handicap) or people with mental health problems. Such people may be viewed as objects of pity and charity; as violent and dangerous; as sick; or as subhuman 'vegetables'. Because of this they have become devalued in society, they are segregated from other people and denied the most basic human rights. They are treated as second-class citizens.

Normalisation . . . suggests ways of offering services which support people in becoming valued members of society. It is not about 'making people normal' — the most common misinterpretation of the principle . . .[2]

People with drug or alcohol problems

Care for these people may involve counselling, treatment programmes or specialist supported housing or homes. Treatment and support may be more directive than in other forms of community care.

People with HIV or AIDS

Care, support and counselling are all vital to people who are HIV positive or who develop AIDS, and their carers. Such people may have some things in common with people who are terminally ill.

People who are terminally ill

Hospice care, with its special emphasis on improving the quality of dying, is most often thought of in relation to cancer patients. However, such care can be relevant for people in the final stages of other illnesses and conditions. It can be provided in a hospice, or in a person's own home. The final stages of

Alzheimer's disease have been called a 'living bereavement' for relatives because of the changed character and heavy care needs of the person suffering from the disease.

Homeless people

People with no permanent address often have difficulty finding help from care services. This could be because they are reluctant to seek help, or because they cannot find anyone willing to care for them. Many single homeless people suffer from mental illness, and the problems of elderly homeless people are increasingly causing concern. Homelessness is the extreme end of housing need. Housing is of great importance for all client groups.

Discrimination in care provision

Lumping people into categories may adversely affect the kind of treatment or services they receive. A person aged over 65 could be physically disabled *and* have a mental illness. If he or she is mainly treated as being 'elderly mentally ill', they may not be thought of as eligible for services which are meant mainly for people who have physical disabilities. Services for people with mental health problems may include counselling, which may not be on offer to people who are labelled as *'elderly* mentally ill'. These are forms of 'age discrimination' or 'ageism'.

Other forms of discrimination have to do with a person's sex or race. It is sometimes wrongly believed that people from black and ethnic minorities do not need services because they 'look after their own'. In most cases, it is much more likely that services are not offered in a way which is understandable to people whose first language is not English, or which are acceptable to people with different customs or religions. Community care services need to guard against such discrimination and cater for all the communities in an area. They should be developed with and by the people who need them. Services imposed on any group of people are likely to be inappropriate.

WHO PROVIDES COMMUNITY CARE?

Carers

We have seen that most community care is provided by family, friends and neighbours. Such people are often referred to as 'informal carers', to distinguish them from people who work in the 'formal' sectors – public, private and voluntary services. However, it should be noted that many carers do not like the use of the word 'informal' to refer to the work they do.

A 1985 survey concluded that some 6 million people offer some form of support to people with care needs; 1.4 million carers offer more than 20 hours per week of care. Of these, 26 per cent are aged 65 and over. Many elderly carers are spouses, and many report that they themselves have some form of long-standing illness.[3]

THE NEEDS OF CARERS

Carers are people of all ages, who support people with an infinite variety of needs. Carers want to be listened to, and believe that their needs must be considered alongside those of the people they care for. They want to be recognised for the contribution they make to the overall pattern of caring.

Some people do not identify themselves as carers. They often feel isolated and unable to ask for help. Others do not wish to be called 'carers', preferring to think of their role as wife or husband, son or daughter.

The work of carers is rarely broken down into the many separate services they offer. Families in particular often provide a full range of services for relatives with care needs. They carry out demanding tasks including nursing, bathing, dressing and lifting. Many help with very intimate caring tasks for people who are paralysed or who cannot move from their beds. Where people are suffering from mental illnesses, families must act as protectors and counsellors. Caring day after day can be exhausting and stressful – sometimes with little or no break – as well as rewarding.

The needs of carers are increasingly understood, mainly because of the work of the Carers National Association, an organisation of carers which has local groups all over the country. However, it can be easy *not* to offer services to someone with a carer on the grounds that they are already being helped and do not need more. This could mean that the carer has to stop caring before he or she really wishes to.

Caring is often seen as a woman's task. Although many older men, in particular, provide care for their wives, some 75 per cent of all carers are women. It is argued that this is because women are *expected* to take on a caring role, particularly for older relatives. In future, however, as the population ages and more women go out to work, it may be that fewer women will be willing or available to be carers.

Carers may also be *users* of community care services, if they have care needs of their own, or if their caring tasks are such that they need help in supporting the person they care for. Carers often give up work, or work shorter hours, in order to be able to care.

The amount and kind of care provided by carers varies enormously, depending on the circumstances of the carer and the person needing care. Friends and neighbours are much less likely to provide a high level of personal care than are 'co-resident' carers – those who live with the person who needs care. Even when people live with someone, their 'network' of support may not be enough for their needs. Their carer may go to work or school, or may simply need extra help. Many families live far from their older relatives. Neighbours who once offered care may move away. 'Occasional' care may be relatively easy to arrange; but as needs increase, friends and relatives may be unable to provide enough.

HOW MUCH FAMILY SUPPORT DO OLDER PEOPLE HAVE?

A high proportion of older people have no families: in 1978 30 per cent of people in Great Britain aged over 75 had never had any children, and 7.5 per cent had outlived their children. In 1988, 50 per cent of all people aged over 75 lived alone. In 1987 61 per cent of women aged over 80 living at home lived alone, with 21 per cent living with children and children-in-law, 11 per cent with their spouse and the other 7 per cent living with other relatives or non-relatives.[4]

'Formal' care providers

Although most community care is in the 'informal' sector, the 'formal' sector provides essential support, through professionals and others who offer particular skills and kinds of care.

The formal sector has several different parts – the 'statutory' or 'public' sector; the 'voluntary' or 'charitable' sector; and the 'private' sector. Sometimes the private and voluntary sectors are lumped together and referred to as the 'independent' sector.

The statutory sector

The statutory sector includes public authorities or bodies which have been created by law and which are paid for mainly through taxes. Statutory provision for community care comes mainly from the National Health Service and from local authorities, in particular the social services and housing departments. Local and health authorities are described in more detail later in this chapter.

Some services are 'directly provided': the authority runs the services itself. Other services are 'indirectly' provided: the authority purchases them from some other organisation or authority. There are charges for many statutory services.

Workers in the statutory sector include community nurses, social workers, home helps and wardens of local authority sheltered housing.

The voluntary sector

The voluntary sector includes charities which provide services or represent particular interests. Voluntary or charitable organisations receive funding from many different sources, including charitable donations, sponsorship, grants from public bodies, and charges for some services. Voluntary sector organisations may provide some services through contracts with public authorities.

Some voluntary organisations are very specialised, for instance the Alzheimer's Disease Society, the National Schizophrenia Fellowship, or Cancer-Link. Each brings together people with particular conditions or problems, or their relatives. Members of local groups share years of experience and have often become expert in a particular type of care. Some groups may provide highly specialised services, staffed by paid workers, or by highly trained volunteers. Other groups form self-help networks to support people with similar interests or needs.

Housing associations (see p 55) often specialise in provision for people with particular needs, such as elderly people with mental illness, or young single homeless people.

It should be noted that the voluntary sector includes both paid and unpaid workers. 'Volunteers' – unpaid workers, or those who receive just an honorarium or expenses – work in all sectors, and continue to form the backbone of voluntary sector work. Many are former professional care workers; others have many years' experience in care work, and increasingly volunteers are trained to carry out complex caring and support work. However, the voluntary sector also makes extensive use of paid specialist workers.

The private sector

The private sector includes companies or individuals offering a wide variety of services. The private sector raises money through its own trading activities – by selling goods or services. Private sector organisations may offer some services through contracts with the public sector. The private sector provides a lot of residential and nursing home care – financed in part by public sector finance, through special rates of income support – and some care for people at home.

The private sector includes large national corporations, which build and provide retirement housing and residential or nursing homes, and much smaller providers such as people who both own and manage care homes and small domestic care agencies. Local and health authorities will increasingly enter into contracts with private organisations to provide some of the care which they decide is necessary in their areas.

Not fitting into any of these categories are the new 'not for profit' organisations. Trusts are being formed, for instance, to take over the management of local authority residential homes.

The local authority

There are several kinds of 'local authority', and people are not always sure who does what. At the time of writing, the system has been in place since local government reorganisation in 1974 (as modified in 1986). However, the Local Government Commission is now undertaking a review of local authorities. It is likely that some counties will be divided into smaller 'unitary' authorities responsible for all local services.

At present, who does what in England depends on whether you live in a county or metropolitan or London borough. A person in a county has *two* 'local authorities': the county council and the district (or borough) council. Examples of counties are Northumberland, Cornwall and Surrey. Districts within those counties are Alnwick, Penwith and Elmbridge. Examples of metropolitan boroughs are Tameside or Sandwell. Southwark is a London borough.

The **county council** is responsible for social services, some education and a range of other services. Counties can be quite large. The work of their social services departments is usually broken down to cover local areas. Other activities, such as planning, may also be 'devolved' to these local areas. Each authority has its own pattern of working.

District (or borough) councils usually cover a town, or several towns. They are responsible for housing, leisure services, environmental health, and a variety of other services. In some areas, district councils have taken responsibility for some social services, such as day care.

In a **metropolitan** or **London borough**, there is just one 'local authority' or council. This is called a 'unitary' authority. It runs social services, housing, some education, and all the other services mentioned above.

Each type of local authority has an elected council which decides within its legal responsibilities how much of which kinds of services the authority will provide. Officers of the various departments are responsible for carrying out the policies of elected members of the council, and for advising them about policy choices. All the activities of the local authority – which is a 'statutory authority' – are carried out through the authority of various Acts of Parliament. These Acts create duties – things the local authority *must* do – and powers – things the local authority *may* do (see p 45). Some Acts which cover community care services are described in Appendix 2.

Health authorities

There are three kinds of health authority: the Regional Health Authority, the District Health Authority, and the Family Health Services Authority (formerly the Family Practitioner Committee) (see box). The National Health Service has been reformed following the 1989 White Paper, *Working for Patients*. New systems of arranging services have been introduced and NHS Trusts have been created which provide NHS services but are not under direct control of the District Health Authority. Many general practitioners (referred to as GP fundholders) have taken on new responsibilities with special new budgets.

HEALTH AUTHORITIES

The Regional Health Authority (RHA) is responsible for overseeing the activities of District Health Authorities (DHAs) and Family Health Services Authorities (FHSAs). Regions are the link between the National Health Service Management Executive (which has been set up by the Government to run the health service) and the DHAs and FHSAs. Regions may advise DHAs and FHSAs about what they expect to see in local plans for health services. It is possible that the role and structure of Regions may change over the next few years.

The DHA is responsible for assessing the health needs of its resident population and arranging care to meet these needs, within the limits of available resources. The DHA can purchase this care from providers, which may include NHS Trusts, units directly managed by the DHA, or private or voluntary providers. The FHSA (formerly the Family Practitioner Committee) is responsible for GPs, dentists, opticians and pharmacists working in the community. The FHSA works with the DHA to assess the health needs of the local population. It has some powers to allocate people to a GP's list, if the person is unable to find a GP.

Some general practices now administer their own budgets: they are responsible for purchasing certain types of health care for their patients, paying for practice staff costs, and paying the costs of medicines for their patients. They are often referred to as GP fundholders.

The Community Health Council (CHC) is not a health 'authority'. It acts as a kind of consumer watchdog for local health services, representing the views of users to the relevant health authorities. It gives information and advice to the public about problems with local health services, and tells people how to make a complaint.

Despite the fact that they often have different boundaries, health and local authorities are expected to work together in planning for community care. However, health authorities are run quite differently from local authorities. Their members are not elected. They are appointed by authority of central government. Co-operation in planning is discussed on pages 56–59.

This chapter has looked at who might need community care, and who might provide it. The rest of the book is about the NHS and Community Care Act and the White Paper *Caring for People*. The next chapter looks briefly at the history of community care and at events leading up to the Act. The following six chapters describe the major areas of change which have been introduced since the Act was passed in 1990.

2 The Development of Community Care

Before looking at the present changes, we should look briefly at the history of community care. History reminds us that there is no 'right' solution to developing good community care. In all probability the current changes will eventually become just another part of a long quest for an elusive ideal.

Several themes have dominated thinking about community care for nearly 40 years. Although the *ideal* of community care is broadly supported by everyone, the *practice* has varied and has often been found to be deficient.

Themes of the *ideal* include:

- the belief that people would rather be cared for in their own homes, or in small homelike places;
- the belief that it is better to care for people out of large institutions, fuelled by evidence that large institutions cannot offer personalised, stimulating environments for either residents or staff;
- a belief in the worth and dignity of each person needing care;
- the belief that reorganisation of services, authorities and professional ways of working will improve services.

Themes of the *practice* include:

- a concern with the high cost of care in institutions, and a belief that care at home is cheaper;
- an inability of different authorities and organisations to work constructively together to improve services;
- the struggle to give priority to care for people with chronic illness or disabling conditions;
- competition between client groups when resources are stretched;

- a conflict between the belief that services are most appropriately planned and provided at local level with the need as seen by successive governments to reduce or tightly control public expenditure;

- a gradual change in the philosophy of public services from 'universal' provision, available as of right and according to need, to 'selective' provision, dependent on means and limited to those in greatest need;

- a change in the philosophy of public social provision to a 'mixed economy', with more emphasis on the private and voluntary sectors as providers;

- a move from support for collective – or state – provision to a belief that individuals should take increasing responsibility for themselves.

THE PROBLEM OF INSTITUTIONALISATION

During the nineteenth century large institutions were built for people with mental illness or mental handicap. People became 'institutionalised' in these hospitals, less able to cope with normal life and dependent on the routine and narrow confines of long-stay institutions.

During the 1950s the nature of such 'institutionalisation' became better understood. The effects of certain mental illnesses could be controlled by new drugs, without the need for hospital treatment. In 1957 the Royal Commission Report on the Law Relating to Mental Illness stated that the time had come for a shift from hospital care to community care. It recommended a 'general reorientation away from institutional care in its present form and towards community care'.

Further evidence about the effects of institutionalisation was collected during the 1960s. In 1962, Peter Townsend surveyed local authority, private and voluntary residential homes. In *The Last Refuge*, he reported that many people in such homes were there not because they needed care, but for other social reasons: homelessness, insufficient home care, lack of resources, or no family to care for them. He found that conditions in homes reduced the autonomy of the residents, and isolated them. In 1969, Pauline Morris, in her book *Put Away*, looked at 'mental subnormality' hospitals. Once again, she found little need for people to be in hospitals, which were isolated and poorly staffed.

In 1969 an inquiry at Ely Hospital investigated the first in a series of scandals involving bad practice in large institutions. This report and others led in the early 1970s to Government White Papers proposing improvements in services for people with mental illness and mental handicap. (A White Paper is an official Government document setting out what the Government proposes to do about a particular issue. It normally leads to a law to bring the changes about.) These documents focused on the need to find ways of enabling people to be cared for in their own homes – or at least out of large institutions. They called for improved co-ordination of services, and for much more support for people in their own homes. The same arguments are still being put forward today.

The first community care plans

In 1962, an ambitious Hospital Plan stated that large mental illness hospitals should gradually be closed and that local authorities should develop more services for people in their own homes and in residential homes. In 1963 local authorities were asked to report on the expected needs of their populations, and their current provision of health and welfare services. These were called the first community care plans, although they differed considerably from the plans we will discuss in Chapter 3. They showed great variations in the provision of services between similar local authorities.

Already, then, some themes were in place: concern about the effects of large institutions, and a realisation that local services varied enormously.

HEALTH AND LOCAL GOVERNMENT REORGANISATIONS

During the 1970s, there was an increasing emphasis on improving the *structures* of authorities and organisations. In 1970, the Local Authority Social Services Act created social services departments as we now know them. The Act took effect in 1972. The idea of setting up social services departments had arisen from a concern about welfare services for children. A committee was set up to look at how social services could be arranged in order to develop an effective *family* service. The Seebohm Report, produced in 1968, then extended the definition of 'the family' beyond the focus on children:

> We could only make sense of our task by considering also childless couples and individuals without any close relatives: in other words, everybody. [5]

The Seebohm Report proposed that personal social services should be brought together into one department, the social services department. This would serve as a single source of help in each local authority for anyone with social care needs. Social workers who had previously specialised in working with children, or with blind people, for instance, were to become 'generic' workers – able to deal with all types of problems.

This reorganisation of social services brought together many 'welfare' services but it also transferred to the National Health Service some of the services that local authorities had traditionally run. Sorting out 'social services' provision thus brought about a firmer split between 'health' and 'welfare' functions. Since then, a major theme of community care policies has been improved co-ordination between health and social services.

The National Health Service was given a new structure in 1974, with revisions in 1982. In 1974 hospital social workers were moved from health authorities to social services. In 1974 local government was also reorganised.

Each of these changes aimed to create *structures* through which better services could be provided. They were based on current thinking about ideal sizes of authorities, and good working practice. Such changes almost always represent some compromise between Government, administrators, professionals and local politicians; in time, they yield to new changes based on different thinking.

The great changes in health and social services during the 1970s took place in the climate of optimism created by a new Act of Parliament, the Chronically Sick and Disabled Persons (CSDP) Act.

The Chronically Sick and Disabled Persons Act 1970

The CSDP Act required local authorities to find out the needs of people in their local populations and to provide certain services for them. These services had to be publicised.

The CSDP Act is still in force today. It has been strengthened by the Disabled Persons (Services, Consultation and Representation) Act 1986. However, then as now, local authorities varied greatly in how they responded to the Act. (Both Acts are described more fully in Chapter 4 (pp 65–66); Appendix 1 describes the provisions of the 1986 Act.)

The hopes which the Act had stimulated gradually gave way to caution about what could be achieved. During the 1970s economic pressures meant that the Government of the day had to restrict public spending by local authorities – even if this meant that they could not fulfil all their duties under various Acts of Parliament.

COMPETING PRIORITIES

Acute and non-acute services

Other pressures affected progress in community care. There was competition for resources in the health service, particularly between acute and non-acute services. Most community care health needs are chronic needs: many people require continuing supervision, or nursing care; many suffer from progressive diseases, such as Parkinson's disease or Alzheimer's disease. Many others face problems because of arthritis or rheumatism or because of the effects of stroke or permanent disablement.

These conditions are not 'glamorous', and it is often argued that they do badly in the competition for resources with acute services. New technology has created wonderful possibilities for treatment, but it has also brought much higher health-care costs. Sometimes the gains have been at the expense of improved services for people with less dramatic needs, which are, however, no less painful or traumatic in their effects.

Different client groups

At about the same time as the hospital scandals, child care also created headlines. The Maria Colwell case in 1974 was followed by a series of child abuse cases which forced social services departments to review their practices with regard to children at risk. Many departments, facing cutbacks in finance, had to reduce their services for other people, particularly bearing in mind that child care services are largely 'mandatory' – they must be provided – while many adult services are not.

These conflicting pressures continue. The 1989 Children Act has placed new responsibilities on social services departments, and some are hard pressed to find the staff and money to meet these new responsibilities, at the same time as improving their support for adults with a wide range of care needs.

More people needing care

Growing numbers of people live in the community and need care. Changes in the structure of the population have meant that striving to improve community care services often seems like running hard just to stand still. In 1941 only 10 per cent of the population was aged over 65, compared with 15.8 per cent today.

DEMOGRAPHY

The study of populations is called demography. One example of demographic change is the increase in the numbers of people aged over 80 or 85, or the increase in the *proportion* of such people compared with the rest of the population. Demography is important in planning for all types of services.

Life expectancy at birth was 48 years for males and 51.6 years for females born in 1906; 58.4 years for males and 62.4 years for females born in 1931; and 66.2 years for males and 71.2 years for females born in 1951. At the same time, the life expectancy remaining to people who have grown old has also increased. In 1906, a man reaching the age of 60 could expect to live another 13.4 years on average; a woman, 14.9 years. In 1981, a man reaching the age of 60 could expect to live another 16.3 years, and a woman, 20.8 years.[6]

The numbers of elderly people have thus grown enormously, and the 'survivors' of earlier years are now living to a very old age. Between 1981 and 2001, the numbers of people aged 85 plus will grow from 600,000 to 1.1 million. Although old age is not a disease, the increase in the ageing population does create new demands for services. So do changes in other groups who need care and support. Where long-stay hospitals have closed, for instance, people have been resettled and require services in the community. Children with learning disabilities are no longer sent to hospital for life – they and their families require support in the community. People with HIV and AIDS form a new group of people needing support.

CONCERN WITH THE COST OF COMMUNITY CARE

The growth in the numbers of elderly people has been accompanied by a change in the method of financing long-term care. Since 1980 special social security help with paying for care in residential and nursing homes has been available to anyone who qualifies on grounds of income and savings, with no assessment of the person's need for a particular type of care. This help was given through special rates of supplementary benefit, and then income support. It is this system which is changing in April 1993, and which is at the root of the community care changes.

In the early 1980s, the benefit was payable according to local limits set by local offices of the Department of Health and Social Security, as it was then called. This led to enormous differences in the amount of benefit paid in different areas, and was considered to be open to abuse. It was said that it led to unnecessarily high fees being charged by some homes. The system was changed in 1985 to a system of national limits for different types of care home, and different categories of care.

The effects of this system began to cause concern in the mid-1980s, when attention focused both on the increasing cost of residential and nursing home care, and on the problems of shifting the balance of care from long-term hospital or residential provision to other types of care.

The 1986 Audit Commission report

In 1981 the Department of Health and Social Security published *Report of a Study on Community Care* which reviewed in some detail the themes we have discussed in this chapter. This report found that there had been 'little identifiable shift in the balance of care for those elderly people on the margin between institutional and community-based care', stressed the importance of close collaboration between health and social services authorities, and noted that ways must be found to shift the balance of resources between the NHS and social services. Following that report, a consultative document was published suggesting how this might be done, but in practice the social security system described above began to affect the distribution of funds for care.

The Audit Commission, an organisation which monitors local government (and now health) expenditure, produced a major report on the subject in 1986.

Making a Reality of Community Care suggested that the availability of supplementary benefit payments for residential and nursing home care was 'skewing' public expenditure for people with care needs. It was too easy for people to go into homes with public support, and this was discouraging the development of effective services for people in their own homes.

Furthermore, the report said, it would cost less in many cases to help people to remain at home, thus reflecting the belief that it is cheaper to help people remain in their own homes than to keep them in institutions.

A warning note on this belief had, however, been sounded in the 1981 report mentioned above:

> For some people community-based packages of care may not always be a less expensive or more effective alternative to residential or hospital provision, particularly for those living alone. In some cases the community alternative might only appear cheap because its level of provision could be considered inadequate.
>
> *Report of a Study on Community Care*, para 3.27

This statement could equally well be made today.

The Griffiths Report

Following the Audit Commission report, the Government asked Sir Roy Griffiths to look at the organisation and funding of community care services. The Griffiths Report – *Community Care: Agenda for action* – has become the baseline for the changes which were described in the 1989 White Paper *Caring for People*, and in the NHS and Community Care Act 1990.

Griffiths was asked

> to review the way in which public funds are used to support community care policy and to advise . . . on the options for action that would improve the use of these funds as a contribution to more effective community care.　　Griffiths Report, p iii, para 2

He said that his report identified 'roadblocks' to the effective planning and delivery of community care services. He proposed that a Minister of State should be 'clearly and publicly identified as responsible for community care' (para 28, p vi). Managers in social services should aim to ensure that 'the right services are provided in good time, to the people who need them most' (p 28).

Griffiths said that people should be helped 'to stay in their own homes for as long as possible, or in as near a domestic environment as possible, so that residential, nursing home and hospital care is reserved for those whose needs cannot be met in any other way' (p 28).

In order to do this, he said that social services authorities must:

(i) have systems which enable them to identify those who have need of care and support in the community;

(ii) assess those needs within the context of the individual's own situation;

(iii) taking account of the views and wishes of the person to be cared for, and any informal carers, decide what packages of care would be best suited to the needs, whether provided directly or indirectly;

(iv) determine the priority to be given to the case, given the total resources available and the competing needs of others;

(v) arrange delivery of the services decided upon;

(vi) keep under review the delivery of that package of services, and the individual's needs and circumstances.   para 3.8

Griffiths proposed that money from central government be specially reserved for local authorities to spend on community care. This would include some money taken from the social security budget, in place of the special benefit for residential and nursing home care. (Reserving money to be spent for a particular purpose is sometimes referred to as 'ring-fencing'.)

People who are able to should pay the full economic cost of services provided in their own homes. People should also be encouraged to plan ahead to meet their own care needs. 'Encouraging those who can afford to plan ahead to do so should help to ensure that public resources are concentrated on those in greatest need' (para 6.60).

Griffiths proposed that local authorities should be required to draw up plans showing how they would co-operate with health and housing authorities to provide services which are broadly in line with Government policy. Services should be provided according to the needs and wishes of individuals and their carers. 'The people receiving help will have a greater say in what is done to help them, and a wider choice' (p 28). The local authority should be the 'lead authority' for this, as it is the democratically elected authority closest to service users.

Although traditionally welfare services are provided mainly by the local authority, Griffiths said that such monopoly provision is not necessarily in the interests of service users: the local authority should become an 'enabler' –

THE WAGNER REPORT

Within a week of the publication of Griffiths' report in 1988, another very important report was published by a committee chaired by Gillian Wagner: *Residential Care: A positive choice*.

The Wagner Report emphasises the positive role of residential care, and the scope for positive choices to be made by residents both on entering such care and while they are in it. Needs for **care** should be separated from needs for **accommodation**: people should not have to move just because their care needs change.

Local authorities should play a lead role in planning accommodation and support services. A statutory duty should be placed on local authorities to propose to individuals a reasonable package of services to enable them to remain at home if that is their choice and it is reasonable to do so.

The report emphasises the rights of the individual as a citizen. Residents of residential homes should have:

a trial period of residence; an agreed contract; access to community services and facilities; privacy; management of their own financial affairs where feasible; access to formalised complaints procedures, supported where appropriate by an advocate or representative.

Staff should have adequate training; *all* homes should be inspected, including those run by the local authority; and the Government should consider bringing nursing homes and residential homes under the same registration and inspection rules.

The Wagner Report's 'five Cs' brought together the principles or values which should form the basis of good practice:

Caring
This should be personal, and residents should feel valued, safe and secure.

Choice
Each resident's right to exercise choice over their daily life should be respected.

Continuity
This includes both consistency of care from staff, and the maintenance of links with a resident's previous life.

Change
For residents, the opportunity for continued development; for staff, a commitment to respond to changing needs.

Common values
Ensuring that practice is based on a shared philosophy and values.

Wagner Report, p 60

acting as the 'designers, organisers and purchasers of non-health care services' (para 1.3.4) and not as monopolistic providers.

Before going on to look at the White Paper *Caring for People*, which incorporated many of Griffiths' recommendations, we should mention the publication of the influential Wagner Report on residential care (see box). Whereas Griffiths had been asked to look at the organisation and funding of care services, Wagner focused on issues of quality and choice – the *ideals* of community care. Her report, too, contributed to the ideas contained in the White Paper.

THE WHITE PAPER: *CARING FOR PEOPLE*

It took the Government about 20 months to prepare its response to Griffiths' and Wagner's reports. The White Paper *Caring for People* was published in November 1989. It set out the framework for the community care changes which the rest of this book is about.

Many – though not all – of Griffiths' and Wagner's recommendations found their way into the White Paper. The Government agreed that the special social security allowances for residential and nursing home care should end, and that the money this would have cost should be given to local authorities to make arrangements for care. But the money should not be 'ring-fenced', as it was thought to be better for local authorities to make their own decisions about how to spend their money. (In October 1992, the Government announced that some of the transferred money would be ring-fenced. This is called the Special Transitional Grant and is described on pp 133–135.)

The Government did not accept the idea of a duty on local authorities to propose 'reasonable' packages of care, as recommended by the Wagner Report. Nor did it accept the need to move towards a unified system of inspection for residential and nursing homes.

The White Paper outlined six **key objectives**, and described seven **key changes** needed to bring about the objectives. The objectives are described in para 1.11 of the document. We will look at each of them in turn.

The six key objectives

Services for people at home

1 'To promote the development of domiciliary, day and respite services to enable people to live in their own homes wherever feasible and sensible. ... In future the Government will encourage the targeting of home-based services on those people whose need for them is greatest.'

Domiciliary, day and respite services are the three key types of services which should help people to stay at home. *Domiciliary* means 'home-based': domiciliary services would include home help, or home care; occupational therapy; and perhaps bathing services. *Day* services include all the different types of daytime care outside a person's home – such as a day centre, luncheon club or day hospital. *Respite* services allow carers and people being cared for to have a break from each other (see box).

RESPITE CARE

A 'respite' means a break. Carers in particular need regular respite, so that they can have time off from caring to pursue their own interests. Respite is also important for the person being cared for, who may welcome a break from being looked after by the same person all the time.

A respite break might be arranged in a person's own home: someone comes in while the carer goes out. Or it could be arranged in a residential home, nursing home or hospital – for instance if the carer goes away on holiday. Some respite care is provided in other people's homes and day centres. Carers need to know that respite care will be available in an emergency, say if they become ill.

This first objective includes the idea of 'targeting'. In the past, it was sometimes said that services were spread too thinly: a lot of people whose needs were not particularly great may have received very little of a service, say an hour or two of home help per week. In future, the Government aims to make best use of resources by encouraging local authorities to 'target' services on the people with the greatest needs. In some areas, this means that home help, for instance, is no longer provided. New 'home care' services are being 'targeted' on people who have care needs as well as a need for help with housework. If people only require help with housework, they may no longer receive a service from the local authority.

Services for carers

2 'To ensure that service providers make practical support for carers a high priority.'

We have already seen that carers – family, neighbours, friends – provide most community care. Such people need recognition and support in order to continue caring. Many need financial help, and consideration of their own needs when assessments for care are being made. They need information about services, and regular, reliable support.

Assessments for care

3 'To make proper assessment of need and good case management the cornerstone of high quality care. Packages of care should then be designed in line with individual needs and preferences.'

A major concern leading to the Griffiths Report was the use of large sums of public money for residential and nursing home care, without proper assessment of need. It has been argued that many people receiving such care might not need it if appropriate services were available in the community. In addition, it has often been said that services provided to people with care needs are picked 'off the shelf' – chosen from what is available, rather than being offered in relation to what the person needs.

A further problem with assessment has been that many different people may carry out assessments. A home care organiser would assess for home care; an occupational therapist would assess for aids within the home; a nurse would assess for the bathing service, and so on. The White Paper aimed to reduce unnecessary duplication and to bring better co-ordination to complex assessments through the social services department.

A 'mixed economy of care'

4 'To promote the development of a flourishing independent sector alongside good quality public services. ... social services authorities should be "enabling" agencies. It will be their responsibility to make maximum possible use of private and voluntary providers.'

The Government believes that a variety of providers will increase choice for service users, and that better services will result from increased competition. Local authorities' community care plans (see Chapter 3) must show how they will encourage independent sector providers. This policy is in line with the Government's aim of reducing the level of public services.

In areas where there has been a long-standing tradition of strong public services, some authorities have been reluctant to encourage provision by other sectors. There may also be areas where the private and voluntary sectors do not wish to develop. There is, for instance, little independent sector residential care in some inner city areas. This will mean that the 'mixed economy of care' will look very different in different local authorities.

A clear demarcation of responsibilities

5   **'To clarify the responsibilities of agencies and so make it easier to hold them to account for their performance.'**

One aim of the White Paper was to make sure that people knew who was responsible for which services. Community care plans should clearly say who will do what. There may be confusion, however, about the division of responsibility between health and local authorities for people with health *and* social care needs. The White Paper states that health authorities' responsibilities remain unchanged under the new community care arrangements – yet local authorities have new responsibilities from April 1993 to assess people who need support from public funds for places in nursing homes, as well as in residential homes. This will lead to negotiation between health and local authorities as to who is responsible for the continuing care of certain people, a subject we discuss more fully on pages 139–141. In the lead-up to 1993, the Government stated that local and health authorities must sort out their respective responsibilities for continuing nursing care in order to qualify to receive the money to be transferred from the social security budget.

Better value for taxpayers' money

6   **'To secure better value for taxpayers' money by introducing a new funding structure for social care. ... social security provisions should not ... provide any incentive in favour of residential and nursing home care.'**

The transfer of Department of Social Security money to local authorities is meant to remove the incentive which previously existed for both health and local authorities to place people in care homes, where they could claim benefit from the Department of Social Security. The issues which this raises are discussed in Chapter 8.

Key changes

To carry out these aims, the White Paper (para 1.12) proposed the following key changes:

1   'Local authorities will become responsible, in collaboration with medical, nursing and other interests, for assessing individual need, designing care arrangements, and securing their delivery within available resources.' (See Chapter 4 on assessment and care management.)

2   'Local authorities will be expected to produce and publish clear plans for the development of community care services, consistent with the plans of health authorities and other interested agencies.' (See Chapter 3 on community care plans.)

3   'Local authorities will be expected to show that they are making maximum use of the independent sector.' (See Chapters 3 and 5 on community care plans and on purchasing and contracting.)

4   'There will be a new funding structure for those seeking public support for residential and nursing home care from April [1993]. After that date local authorities will take responsibility for financial support of people in private and voluntary homes, over and above general social security entitlements. The new arrangements will not, however, apply to people already resident in homes before April [1993]', who will continue under the existing system. (See Chapter 8 on paying for care.)

5   'Applicants with few or no resources of their own will be eligible for the same levels of Income Support and Housing Benefit, irrespective of whether they are living in their own homes or in independent residential or nursing homes.'

People who enter private and voluntary care homes from 1 April 1993 will have access to a new residential allowance as part of income support. This replaces the reference to Housing Benefit in the White Paper. The new allowance is explained on page 130.

The Government has deliberately withheld support for housing costs through the residential allowance from people in homes directly run by the local authority: it wants local authorities to encourage independent sector care homes, and has thus ensured that the local authority will pay more from its own funds for people cared for in its own homes.

6 'Local authorities will be required to establish inspection and registration at arms-length from the management of their own services which will be responsible for checking on standards in both their own homes and in independent sector residential care homes.'

The Government accepted the Wagner Report's recommendations that local authority homes should be inspected, but rejected the recommendation that new independent inspectorates should be responsible for both residential and nursing homes. The responsibility for inspecting all residential homes therefore rests with the local authority, but inspection must be separate – at 'arms-length' – from the authority's management of its own homes. (See Chapter 7 on inspection.)

7 'There will be a new specific grant to promote the development of social care for seriously mentally ill people.'

The Government recognised that social services expenditure for people with mental health problems was often only a small part of a local authority's budget. It therefore proposed to create a separate, special grant, which, unlike most local authority money for community care, would be 'ring-fenced' specially for projects for people with mental health problems. Local authorities must add some money of their own to the grant, and must agree on the projects with their local health authorities. A special grant for services for people with drug and alcohol problems was introduced later.

The White Paper also proposed that local authority social services departments should set up new complaints procedures (see Chapter 6).

At first, the Government proposed that the community care changes should all take place by April 1991. This allowed very little time between the publication of the White Paper and full implementation of the changes. An Act of Parliament was needed to make the necessary changes in the law – in addition to those needed for the reorganisation of the National Health Service, which was taking place at the same time. The NHS and Community Care Act became law in June 1990. In July 1990, the Government announced that the changes would not take place all at once. They would be phased in between 1991 and 1993.

The NHS and Community Care Act 1990

Changes in the law were necessary for some of the recommendations in the White Paper. These included:

— amending the National Assistance Act 1948, to allow local authorities to make arrangements for people to be cared for in nursing homes, as well as in residential homes (section 42);

— creating a duty for local authorities to prepare community care plans in consultation with health and housing authorities, and with certain voluntary organisations (section 46);

— creating a duty (in addition to their existing duty to assess under the Disabled Persons Act 1986) for local authorities to assess people who may be in need of community care services and to decide whether these needs call for provision by them of such services (section 47);

— creating an additional power for local authorities to inspect their own residential homes, and other community care services provided or arranged by them (section 48);

— giving the Secretary of State powers to direct local authorities to carry out certain social services tasks, including the setting up of complaints procedures and the provision of new grants for mental illness and drug and alcohol problems; and giving 'default powers' to the Secretary of State to order a local authority to carry out certain duties, if it has failed to carry out these duties with respect to social services (section 50).

POWERS AND DUTIES

Local authorities have *powers* and *duties*. A power is something they are able to do, but do not have to. They have the power, for instance, to provide recreation and leisure services. However, they have a *duty* to provide certain social services — for instance, they must provide residential care for people who need it and for whom it is not otherwise available (under the 1948 National Assistance Act); and certain social services for disabled people (under the Chronically Sick and Disabled Persons Act 1970).

There are no set amounts of the services which authorities must provide under these statutory duties. Each case must be judged individually.

The Government has issued Guidance to local authorities about carrying out the community care changes. The Policy Guidance (*Community Care in the*

Next Decade and Beyond) tells local and health authorities what is expected of them if they are to meet the Government's proposals on community care. The Policy Guidance covers all aspects of the community care changes.

Practice Guidance has also been issued by the Department of Health on most aspects of the changes. It covers in much more detail what local authorities might do in carrying out each part of the changes.

The idea of community care is not new. Different *ideals* of community care have been pursued for nearly 40 years. Themes of these years have included concern about quality and availability of care, coupled with a desire to get the 'system' right, to develop the roles of professional workers, and to limit public spending. The aim of developing community care for people at home has been rooted in the belief that such care is preferable for and desired by most people. It has been believed (but not confirmed) to be cheaper than care in institutions.

The rest of this book looks at the main changes which are being introduced as part of the community care changes. It looks in more detail at the White Paper, the 1990 Act and the Government's Policy and Practice Guidance.

3 Community Care Plans

Planning is – or should be – the activity which underpins most work. Yet it is easy to pass over in a hurry. Too often we are impatient to get on with the job, thinking it a waste of time to stop to make a plan – to set aims and objectives; to consider what resources we have and how we can best use them; to check on what we are doing, revising our plans in the light of the information we receive.

The community care changes recognise this reluctance by creating a duty in law for local authorities to prepare community care plans. This chapter sets out what the 1990 Act said about plans, and looks at the Government's Guidance to local authorities.

HOW SHOULD THE PLANS BE DRAWN UP?

The White Paper and the Act

The White Paper, *Caring for People*, said that local authorities must prepare community care plans, which should state objectives and priorities for community care, and set specific targets for meeting these. The plans must be made public, and must link with the community care plans of other authorities – the housing department, the District Health Authority and the Family Health Services Authority.

WHAT THE 1990 NHS AND COMMUNITY CARE ACT SAID ABOUT PLANNING

Section 46 states that local authorities must follow the directions of the Secretary of State to prepare and publish a community care plan, keep the plan under review, and change it or produce a new one if they are directed to do so by the Secretary of State. They must consult any District Health Authority and Family Health Services Authority which is in their area. If they are not a housing authority, they must consult the housing authority, if the plan may affect or be affected by the provision or availability of housing. They must also consult voluntary housing agencies, and voluntary organisations which represent users of services or their carers. (The Government has since issued a direction to make consultation with local independent supplier representatives a concrete legal obligation.)

The local authority – the county, metropolitan borough, or London borough – is the 'lead authority' in community care planning. It should bring together all the main service providers and produce an agreed plan, showing who will do what.

Health authorities are also expected to prepare plans showing their community care policies. They can do this by themselves, or as part of the local authority community care plan.

The Government's Policy Guidance describes how local and health authorities should tackle the planning task. It gives guidance on how different authorities should co-operate with each other in preparing plans, and how the Social Services Inspectorate of the Department of Health will look at the plans, and give advice and guidance on them. District Health Authority plans will be checked on by the Regional Health Authority.

WHAT SHOULD THE PLANS CONTAIN?

The following is a summary from the Policy Guidance (para 2.25) of what social services departments should show in their community care plans:

- a summary of the needs of the local population and the client groups for whom they intend to arrange services;

- a description of existing services, how priorities will be chosen, how social services departments intend to offer practical help, such as respite care, to carers, and how they plan to develop services for people at home;

- how quality in providing and purchasing services will be ensured and checked on (and what part inspection units and complaints procedures will play in this);

- how they intend to increase consumer choice and stimulate the development of a mixed economy of care;

- how much their plans will cost, what staff will be needed, and how money and staff will be used most effectively;

- how the authority has consulted with others in preparing plans;

- how it plans to tell service users and carers about services, and when the next plan will be published.

The plans should also describe how other aspects of the community care changes will be carried out – how inspection units and complaints procedures will work and how the whole process will be monitored.

In autumn 1992, the Government (in the 'Foster-Laming' letter) set out a range of 'key tasks' which local and health authorities must carry out before April 1993. Community care plans for 1993 should reflect these by showing:

- what resources health and local authorities expect to devote to community care in 1992–93 and 1993–94;

- services expected to be available, and changes planned for existing services;

- details of assessment arrangements;

- arrangements for purchase of residential and nursing home care;

- charging policies and arrangements for financial assessments;

- details of agreements between health and local authorities, particularly those for purchase of nursing home care, assessment arrangements and hospital discharge;

- details of agreements with housing authorities;

- how the plan has taken account of new GP fundholder purchasing responsibilities;

- how client choice will be taken into account;

- how the public will be informed about local implementation of the 1993 changes.[7]

Much of what is in the plans relates to subjects discussed in other chapters of this book. Here we look at some of the planning tasks in a little more detail.

Assessing the needs of the population

For planning purposes, 'needs assessment' means finding out about the care needs of local people. (It has another meaning in the context of assessment and care management (see Chapter 4), where it refers to the assessment of an individual person's needs.)

Local authorities have been assessing the needs of their populations for a long time. In 1970 the Chronically Sick and Disabled Persons Act required authorities to discover the needs of disabled people in their areas, and to provide certain services for them. Many local authorities were hard pressed to develop an accurate picture of need, and for most it was virtually impossible to keep such information up to date.

It should in theory be easier now for local authorities to find out about local needs, and to build up profiles of the different client groups. New systems of information management should help authorities keep track of needs. Records can show who uses services, and what users think about them. Just as important, information can be collected about people who need services but do not use them. Over time, the aim is for authorities to develop a much better picture of who needs what in their areas.

Sir Roy Griffiths commented on the importance of good information systems in local authorities, and noted that at the time of his report, such systems needed considerable improvement. Much effort has since been devoted to developing ways of gathering and using information about community care needs.

Special factors

In assessing the needs of their local populations, the Policy Guidance said that local authorities should be looking out for special factors which may affect needs for community care – for instance the needs of people in rural or inner city areas.

It will be useful to reflect for a moment on the sometimes neglected subject of rural needs. In some counties, up to 50 per cent of people live in the country. Yet many of the services they need are likely to be in towns, including doctors, dentists, opticians and hospitals, as well as mainstream shopping and leisure facilities.

A voluntary worker: 'The elderly people living here have lived an almost feudal existence. Many have lived all their lives in small villages where they have worked for the big house or farm in tied cottages with low wages. Then the Post Office closes, the village store and school go, the young people emigrate. Buses are "uneconomic" and the doctor has relocated. They need to make a journey for every single thing they want.'

Local authority plans will need to show how the special needs of rural populations will be met, taking into account housing, health and transport provision as well as social services.

The numbers of homeless or transient people will also be important for planning, as will the needs of people from black and ethnic minority communities.

A London borough's 1992 community care plan presents evidence that members of black and ethnic minority communities are disproportionately represented among the most disadvantaged groups suffering unemployment, homelessness, poor housing conditions and the effects of disability, sickness and higher than average mortality rates. 'It is significant that much of the current information about available services is failing to reach this group of people and therefore has prevented them from having their needs met.'

To combat the problem, the borough has set out steps for development. These include: 'a language policy; a disability strategy; drawing up new consultation guidelines; grant aid to the black and ethnic minority voluntary sector; recruitment of specialist staff; monitoring service delivery to ethnic minority users; and talking with members of ethnic minority communities about services appropriate to their needs and how best to publicise them.'[8]

In order to check on these various special needs, the authority will need to make sure that its consultation process allows different groups of people to express their views, as well as using facts and figures already available.

Consultation

Consultation is often talked about, but is not easy to do well. It needs to reach different groups of people, large and small. It must ensure that people understand what they are being consulted about, and that they have enough information about what is going on to comment both on existing services and on those they would like to see developed. It has to be able to take on board many different points of view – of individuals and the organisations representing them, and of service providers and planners in all sectors.

If it is not to be just a 'paper exercise', the consultation process must show that it has responded to what was said – explaining, where necessary, why certain views have not been acted on. It needs to be an ongoing exercise, not just a one-off performance.

Seeking the views of users is an important part of consultation. In addition, consultation should include potential users who may not be using services now, perhaps because:

— they don't want to;
— they don't know about services, or they can't get out to find out about them;
— there isn't enough of a particular service to go round;
— they can't afford the charges;
— they live in sheltered or supported homes, where it is assumed that they will receive support;
— they have relatives, friends or neighbours who provide the necessary help – carers, who, as we have seen, may be users themselves.

Efforts have to be made to contact those who might not easily learn about the process. This means that information about plans should be available, affordable and understandable to all possible users, including:

— people who can't get out of their homes;
— people who are blind and/or deaf;
— people who don't speak or read English;
— people who can't use public transport;
— people who don't understand social services jargon.

In preparing their first plans, some authorities made great efforts to consult local people, holding open days, providing transport to meetings, offering respite support to enable carers to take part, and consulting users of day centres and other services. In other authorities, consultation was patchy and not well thought through: not enough notice was given of meetings, and the people being consulted did not have adequate information about what was being proposed

Response to consultation often varied between client groups. In some areas older people are not used to being consulted, or to expressing their views.

A planner: 'We found it difficult to identify the "elderly consumer". We held two days for elderly people, but by and large those who came were the workers who cared for them, such as nurses. We did encourage them to bring clients and carers, but generally they didn't come.'

Users may need help to learn how to express their views, and to learn how to take part in planning, so that they can be fully involved and not always have to rely on others to put their point of view. Authorities may have to learn how to set up consultation so that users feel able to take part.

Trying to meet users' needs

One *dilemma* for local authorities is the problem of raising expectations. If everyone is encouraged to say what they need, there are bound to be disappointments if all the needs cannot be met.

A planner: 'Our members [the Council] said this plan was full of expectations – we shouldn't raise expectations which cannot be met. But disabled people said to us, "How dare you not discuss our unmet needs with us?" Our committee will have to learn to tolerate the concept of unmet need, and to debate this with the people in need.'

Acting on the views of users will inevitably involve compromise. It is clearly impossible to plan for every single person's individual needs – and different groups of service users may want very different things. But the aim is to move towards services that meet the needs of users, rather than services that are provided for the convenience of those who organise them, or to match what professionals say people ought to want. The planning process is a crucial part of this.

Consultation must also involve other authorities and service providers from all sectors. After preparation of their first plans in 1992, many local authorities appeared to have succeeded in consulting local interests effectively, but some were criticised for not consulting adequately with other sectors. A report commissioned by the Department of Health in the spring of 1992[9] showed that in many areas the private sector had not been much involved in consultation about plans. This sometimes occurred because there was no clear local organisation to consult, but also at times reflected local authorities' reluctance to work with private sector providers.

In general, voluntary organisations had been more involved, but many felt that local authority timescales for consultation were unrealistic, and that inadequate information had been provided. Others felt that no action had been taken on the views they expressed.

The Government has stated that it wishes local authorities to consult fully with *all* sectors, and has issued a direction to give local authorities a legal obligation to consult with local independent sector supplier representatives on the community care plans for April 1993.

At its best, consultation means the local authority taking account of and acting on the views of local people and organisations representing a wide range of interests. At its worst, it is simply something which must be 'gone through' in order to fulfil the requirements of the planning exercise.

Making an inventory

One of the first steps in community care planning is to sort out who does what: to make an inventory. To achieve this, co-operation is needed *within* the local authority as well as with the private and voluntary sectors and other statutory authorities.

A county council in the Midlands wants to bring together all its departments and those of its districts to make a special effort to develop its community care services. 'Involving all Departments is important because good quality community care includes a range of services, such as transport, employment, housing, libraries, education as well as those provided by Social Services. People with special needs should have equal access to all these services.'[10]

For older people housing and transport are often particularly important.

Housing and community care planning

Caring for People refers briefly to the importance of housing, stating:

> If dependent people are to be helped to continue living in the community, then their homes must be places where it is possible to provide the care they need. The Government believes that housing is a vital component of community care and is often the key to independent living. para 3.5.1

The White Paper went on to say: 'Social services authorities will need to work closely with housing authorities, housing associations and other providers of housing of all types in developing plans for a full and flexible range of housing' (para 3.5.4).

Housing services may be provided by the local authority, or by housing associations. Private providers increasingly offer different types of retirement housing for purchase.

HOUSING ASSOCIATIONS

Housing associations are non-profit-distributing organisations run by voluntary committees. Some cater for general needs, while others are more specialist. For instance, some organisations have special projects of and for people from black and ethnic minority groups.

The type of care arranged by housing associations is very varied, ranging from shared housing, where people have their own rooms but some shared facilities, to staffed hostels, sheltered accommodation and residential care.

Local authorities and housing associations can provide a place for people to move *to* – for instance from an unmodernised home with stairs to a ground-floor flat with special adaptations, or from a long-stay hospital to a group home. Local authorities can also provide help to improve or adapt a person's existing home. In some areas there is a home improvement agency service, sometimes called Staying Put or Care and Repair, which gives advice and practical assistance to people who need to repair, improve or adapt their homes. These schemes are run by local authorities, housing associations, and a variety of voluntary organisations.

Despite the importance of housing to community care, many of the first community care plans gave it scant coverage. In September 1992 the Departments of the Environment and of Health issued a joint circular on housing and community care (DOE 10/92; LAC(92)12). This circular stressed the importance of co-operation between housing and social services authorities in preparing plans and in assessment procedures. The 'Foster-Laming' letter (see p 49) emphasised the need for housing to have a much higher profile in community care plans.

Transport and community care planning

The crucial role played by transport in community care is acknowledged in the Practitioners' Guide, part of the Department of Health's Practice Guidance on assessment (see p 67):

[Transport] is fundamental in enabling services to get to people or people to services. Failure to recognise its contribution can lead to false perceptions of need, for example, providing meals on wheels to someone who fails to cook because they have no means of reaching the shops. *Practitioners' Guide*, p 59

Effective transport helps people to reach services – such as day care, day hospitals and outpatients departments. It is also important that carers and relatives should be able to visit people being cared for away from their own homes. For many people transport also provides the link with 'ordinary' life – shops, libraries, cinemas and other recreational facilities.

Although largely ignored in the first community care plans, transport needs to be considered in inventories of local services in order to plan effectively for community care.

A planner from a local authority: 'The housing department's plan is included in the community care plan; but transport is still a gap – there isn't a policy on that.'

Negotiating planning agreements

Another task for the local authority is to negotiate planning agreements with local health authorities. These agreements will be statements that they have agreed common goals for services, have made funding agreements, and have decided who will do what.

Such planning agreements will be an essential part of community care in any local area. They should ensure that disputes do not arise between health and local authorities. If, for example, a local authority wants to increase the numbers of elderly people who can be cared for in their own homes, it may make arrangements for sitting services to relieve carers, for day care, and for social work support for older people and their families. At the same time, the authority will rely on the relevant health authority or fundholding GP to arrange appropriate nursing services, incontinence provision and physiotherapy. There will need to be agreement about how this will work.

In Chapter 2 we described some of the complexities of local and health authority structures. Many social services and health authorities are not 'coterminous'. In other words, they do not have the same boundaries. There may be several health authorities within one local authority, or a health authority may cover part of several metropolitan boroughs. In addition to having different boundaries, the various authorities have their own customs, cultures and organisational structures, so one local authority may be dealing with several very different health authorities. Local health services are also becoming very complex, as the number of NHS Trusts increases, and greater numbers of fundholding GPs assume responsibilities for certain community health and other services for their patients.

JOINT WORKING: HEALTH AND SOCIAL SERVICES

Planning agreements will be made easier by the existence in some areas of joint working, through Joint Consultative Committees or Joint Care Planning Teams. Such bodies bring together health and social services officers and workers to promote co-operative working – either in the authorities as a whole or, for instance, with reference to a particular client group, such as elderly people, people with learning disabilities or people with mental health problems.

Joint finance is often used for projects run by the NHS, social services or voluntary organisations, but involving co-operation and budget-sharing between them. This is a way of crossing the sometimes artificial barriers between health and social services.

All this makes the negotiation of planning agreements a complex task. From 1993 such agreements must cover the assessment of care needs, the provision of continuing care, including respite care, in residential and nursing homes, and training strategies – Government Guidance encourages the development of joint training between authorities and organisations.

The Managers' Guide (see p 67) on care management and assessment discusses what may be involved. It notes that the 1990 Act places a formal duty on local authorities to bring apparent health care needs to the attention of the appropriate health authority, and states that 'health professionals are expected to identify social care needs and advise patients appropriately. Community care plans should spell out how the two agencies will put this duty into effect' (para 4.17).

The Managers' Guide goes on to discuss the negotiation which will be involved in devising collaborative care management and assessment procedures – which will affect community care planning:

In England, local authorities will have to engage with both District Health Authorities and Family Health Service [sic] Authorities as the purchasing authorities. There may also be direct negotiation between local authorities and provider units, such as NHS Trusts, where these offer social care facilities. The way that fundholding general practitioners deploy their budgets may also have an impact on the profile of community care services at the local level so they, too, should be party to such negotiations.   para 4.18

Negotiating planning agreements will require health and local authorities to face the difficult task of defining their respective responsibilities for 'health' and 'social' care.

Sir Roy Griffiths said that health authorities should provide for 'health' not 'social' needs. This view has been confirmed by the Government:

> In relation to community care, health care involves the investigation, diagnosis, treatment and rehabilitation undertaken by a doctor or by other professional staff to whom a doctor has referred the patient. In addition, it includes health promotion and the prevention of ill health.
>
> Social care consists of non-health care and support provided through the supply of goods and services to maintain or establish people in their own homes, or by residential or non-acute nursing home care, as appropriate to individuals' needs.[11]

In practice, distinguishing between health and social care is not always easy. Home helps or home carers often carry out 'nursing' tasks, such as administering drugs, changing catheters, or changing dressings and colostomy bags. Bathing services are often disputed territory between health and social services, as noted in a report from Age Concern Greater London:

> Few would argue with the premise that to keep oneself clean is a fundamental need and not a luxury . . . Elderly people who cannot bath themselves appear to be falling through a gap between their health authority district nursing service and their local authority social services, with neither authority willing to admit responsibility for running the service.[12]

The National Association of Health Authorities and Trusts (NAHAT) has published a report describing a project which attempted to define 'health' and 'social' tasks. It emphasised the importance of avoiding disputes about who should do what, while stressing the need to identify who should be responsible, and who should pay for different services. The working party which prepared the report defined a range of tasks as part of 'health' or 'social' care and some tasks as 'both/either'. It recognised that such definitions will be useful as a guide, 'but will not resolve all of those very difficult situations where there is inter-authority disagreement about responsibilities for a number of particular individual cases'.[13]

A social services officer: 'To me I don't think it's where medical services end or social services begin. Because I don't think you can package people. But there are grey areas in between, and I think we have to work together to find out where they are. A lot of people are on the edges of health and social care. Their needs can change from one to the other and we have to allow ourselves not to be constricted by artificial divisions.'

To break down some of the barriers between 'health' and 'social' care, Griffiths referred in his report to the creation of a new type of worker – a 'community carer'. He suggested that community carers might take on the work of some home helps or home care assistants, community nursing assistants and residential care staff (Griffiths Report, para 8.4).

However such work is done, the Managers' Guide for care management and assessment makes clear that negotiations at local level will be crucial:

> The Government has not thought it appropriate to attempt to define a rigid demarcation between health and social care; the interface between the two is for local discussion and agreement.   para 4.20

It is to avoid potential disputes that the Government has urged health and local authorities to make clear planning agreements showing who will do what. Indeed, for nursing home provision, the Government has *required* local authorities to show how they have reached agreement with health authorities about their respective responsibilities as a condition of receiving funds transferred from the social security budget in 1993.

Setting targets

The planners should define aims and objectives for services and set *measurable targets* for services to aim for, and time limits for meeting them. These can be genuine expressions of new goals, although in practice they may often amount to not much more than vague statements of good intentions. Targets might include:

— ensuring that everyone assessed as being of a particular dependency level has access to a certain amount of services;

— achieving a certain staffing level for services;

— providing a certain number of day care places;

— improving co-operation between services;

— preparing a report on one aspect of services, such as enhancing equality of opportunity.

The limitation of targets is that they tend to relate to easily measurable aspects of a service – for instance, the number of home carers per 1,000 people aged over 75. Even if you know this target has been met, this will not necessarily tell you how *good* the service is. Targets cannot tell you much about the *quality* of services, unless they include a way of measuring quality as well as quantity – such as interviewing a certain number of service users to find out how they feel about the service in question.

Choosing priorities

Setting targets means choosing priorities. We have seen that one of the Government's main aims is to ensure that services are as effective and as efficient as possible in meeting needs, given the resources that are available. This means that some needs will be identified which cannot be met. Part of the purpose of the consultation process, and of negotiating with everyone involved, will be to decide which needs should have greatest priority.

A major aim of the White Paper is that services should be *targeted* on those in greatest need. How such need is identified locally will depend on the priorities chosen, but must take into account the statutory duties which local authorities already have to provide certain services (see p 45). There is no hard and fast rule about how priorities are set. This is one reason why a good consultation process is so important. Without one, the priorities chosen may simply reflect the needs of those who shout the loudest, perhaps neglecting the needs of vulnerable but less vocal people.

The targeting dilemma

There is a dilemma here. Targeting services seems to make good sense. It should direct resources where the needs are greatest. For older people, this is often said to mean those who are at risk of having to leave their own homes because of growing care needs. Targeting resources on such people may help them remain at home as long as possible, but may be at the expense of people with lower levels of need who were formerly receiving some help.

Many authorities are already well down the road to increased 'targeting'. Their plans illustrate moves towards providing more intensive services to fewer people. Some former users of services have been very much taken by surprise when their service has been withdrawn. One woman wrote to the social services department about her mother, aged 93, whose home help was withdrawn, despite health problems:

I note that services have been cut by 25 per cent. Twenty-five per cent of four hours per week, the service my mother was receiving, is one hour, leaving three hours per week. Perhaps you can explain why my mother's service has been cut by 100 per cent! . . . I feel you are particularly shortsighted. In my mother's case, you could, with a little more thought and organisation, have cut her service by 50 per cent not 100 per cent. As it is, if this coming winter is anything like the last, my mother may have to apply for residential care, at a time when I was under the impression you would rather keep people in their own homes with help.

A home care organiser: 'There are changed criteria now because of the budget. There's no preventive work done, and if you don't do the preventive work, the person becomes a crisis. If you take the service away and if the family don't come in (and a lot of elderly people don't have a family) you've got a crisis.'

Some people are concerned that focusing mainly on the people with the greatest needs will lead to neglect of those who have *some* care needs, but who are not yet *very* dependent. It could be that those who can afford to will be able to buy in services for themselves, leaving less well off people unable to buy services and unable to obtain them from the local authority. It is early days yet to say whether this will happen. It is important to remember that some such people may have rights under the Chronically Sick and Disabled Persons Act (see pp 65–66).

MONITORING AND REVIEW

All aspects of the community care changes should feed back into a monitoring and review system. Like planning, monitoring and review should really be part of most kinds of work. Also like planning, it is easy to neglect this. Frequently, service providers who think they do a good job do not see the point of monitoring and reviewing what they do. They can get stuck in a particular pattern if they do not constantly check on how they are doing and think about ways of improvement.

Local authorities will be required to monitor and review their community care plans each year. This should mean that they look at all parts of their community care work, drawing on the information they obtain from, for instance, the consultation, inspection and complaints processes, or from checking on how their contracts are working out. It is likely in the early years that the monitoring and review process will show gaps in service provision – partly because many authorities simply have not kept track of things in this way before.

At a national level, community care plans will be monitored by the Department of Health's Social Services Inspectorate. It will publish regional reports about how all the community care changes are working, and offer advice and guidance to local authorities whose plans do not look like meeting the key objectives of the White Paper over a reasonable time. If necessary, it will advise the Secretary of State for Health, who has the power under the NHS and Community Care Act to intervene to make sure that 'local authorities' plans are in line with national policies and priorities, and that implementation is proceeding at a reasonable pace' (Policy Guidance, para 2.21).

The monitoring and review process offers everyone concerned – service users, carers, voluntary and private providers, and local taxpayers – a chance to have their say about how they think things are working. The consultation process, the assessment procedure, and the complaints and inspection processes provide other such opportunities. A record should be kept of how people feel about what is provided – or about what they feel they need. This record should be made publicly available, and will give users and others in the community better information through which to exercise their powers as citizens.

They may want to try to persuade the relevant authorities to put resources into new initiatives, or they may find that there simply are not enough resources available. They may then want to contact their local Member of Parliament and the Government of the day, to lobby for more resources to be made available from central funds. Every four years they will be able to vote on who runs their local authority services.

This chapter has shown that local authorities are now required by law to prepare community care plans in co-operation with health and, where appropriate, housing authorities. The plans should be easy to understand and include information about services for different client groups and about how help will be offered to carers.

If the plans are to be useful to local people, they must know that such plans exist, and where to find them. They will need to be able to find out what has happened to proposals in the previous plan, and how consultation will be carried out for the next one. In this way, the community care plans will be the beginning and end of the yearly cycle of planning for and providing services.

4 Assessment and Care Management

One aim of the community care changes is to make sure that publicly supported services are provided on the basis of a proper assessment of needs. Assessment is the first step in the process of care management – of sorting out needs, deciding whether services can be arranged, devising a 'package of care' in a 'care plan', and reviewing the situation from time to time.

In this chapter we look at assessments and the whole process of care management.

LOCAL AUTHORITIES' LEGAL DUTIES

The White Paper and the Act

Caring for People spelt out the duty of local authorities to assess people needing 'social care and support – eg for mobility, personal care, domestic tasks, financial affairs, accommodation, leisure and employment, which they cannot arrange for themselves' (para 3.2.2).

> Assessment should take account of the wishes of the individual and his or her carer, and of the carer's ability to continue to provide care . . . efforts should be made to offer flexible services which enable individuals and carers to make choices.
>
> *Caring for People*, para 3.2.6

The NHS and Community Care Act made assessment of need for 'community care services' a duty for local authorities. Where it appears to an authority that 'any person for whom they may provide or arrange for the provision of community care services may be in need of any such services' the authority must carry out an assessment of needs for services and decide whether these needs call for provision of such services (section 47(1)(a) and (b)).

Community care services are those which local authorities can provide under the following Acts: Part III of the National Assistance Act; section 45 of the Health Services and Public Health Act 1968; section 21 of and Schedule 8 to the National Health Service Act 1977; and section 117 of the Mental Health Act 1983. (These are described in Appendix 2.)

This duty to assess is linked with the transfer of social security funds to local authorities, and is meant to ensure that publicly supported care in homes is provided on the basis of an assessment of need. Assessment should also identify people who can best be helped to remain in their own homes, with appropriate support.

Who will be eligible for assessment?

People who 'appear to need community care services' will be eligible. Local authorities must publish information about eligibility for assessment and for services (Policy Guidance, para 3.18). This information should be prepared in co-operation with health and housing authorities, and with other service providers. It should include:

— how and where to apply for an assessment;

— who is eligible for assessment;

— how the authority will decide who is eligible for services;

— how to make representations and complaints;

— details about the care services available in residential and nursing homes and in people's own homes, provided by all sectors.

The information should be available to anyone who needs it, and should take account of the needs of people who do not speak English, who have various cultural backgrounds, or who have difficulty communicating.

Each local authority will have its own system for assessment and provision of services. This means that people living in different parts of the country will be covered by different procedures – with the exception of the charging procedures for residential and nursing home care (see pp 129–131).

The existing rights of disabled people

If, during an assessment under the 1990 Act, an authority finds that a person should be considered as a 'disabled person', the NHS and Community Care Act states that the authority must also assess the person under the provisions of the Disabled Persons (Services, Consultation and Representation) Act 1986, and tell the person about their rights under that Act. In order to understand the provisions of that Act, it is necessary to look briefly at some earlier legislation. The National Assistance Act defines the people who are eligible for services under the Chronically Sick and Disabled Persons Act.

The National Assistance Act 1948

Section 29 of the National Assistance Act 1948, as amended, gave local authorities a general duty to promote the welfare of certain people. They were defined (in England) as:

> Persons aged 18 or over who are blind, deaf or dumb or who suffer from mental disorder of any description and other persons aged 18 or over who are substantially and permanently handicapped by illness, injury or congenital deformity or such other disabilities as are described by the Minister. [DHSS Circular LAC(74)13, para 11, stated that 'partially sighted or hard of hearing' people should also be included in this definition.]

The Chronically Sick and Disabled Persons Act 1970

The Chronically Sick and Disabled Persons (CSDP) Act 1970 describes the services to be provided under this general duty more specifically. Section 2 lists services to be provided where the local authority is 'satisfied' that they are needed and that they will meet the needs of the disabled person. In summary, they are:

— practical assistance in the home;

— provision of, or assistance in obtaining, radio, television, library or similar recreational facilities;

— recreational facilities outside the home, or help in taking advantage of educational facilities;

— facilities for, or assistance in, travelling to and from home to participate in any services provided by the local authority under section 29 of the National Assistance Act, or similar services (eg sheltered employment);

C

- assistance in arranging for any works of adaptation in the home or the provision of additional facilities designed to secure greater safety, comfort or convenience;
- facilities for taking holidays;
- meals at home or elsewhere;
- provision of, or assistance in obtaining, a telephone and any special equipment necessary to enable use of a telephone.

The Act also requires local authorities to find out how many disabled people live in their area and to keep a register of such people. Being registered with the local authority under this Act is what we mean when we talk about someone being 'registered as disabled', but people do not have to be 'registered' in order to receive services under the Act.

The Disabled Persons Act 1986

Section 4 of the Disabled Persons (Services, Representation and Consultation) Act 1986 then gave local authorities a duty to assess people for services which could be provided under the CSDP Act, if asked to do so by the disabled person, his or her representative, or a carer. Section 8 requires the local authority, when making an assessment, to consider the ability of a carer to continue to provide care on a regular basis. (See Appendix 1.)

The new community care assessment process must take account of people's rights under these Acts.

The new legislation

Local authorities thus already had a duty to assess the individual needs of disabled people when requested, and to provide certain services for them. The 1990 Act adds to this by saying that a disabled person must be assessed under that Act *without* the authority being requested to do so, and that people who appear to need community care services must also be assessed.

None of the Acts shows how 'needs' should be defined, nor are there stated levels of service which should be provided under the authority's various legal duties. This means that the variation in provision which has always existed between authorities will continue, and that it is difficult to say how much of a particular service should be available for a particular person.

Despite the fact that we do not have hard and fast ways of judging if, or how much of, a service should be available, we can look at what the Government has said about local authorities setting up assessment and care management processes. We have already mentioned the Policy Guidance, which says what is expected of local authorities. The Practice Guidance gives much more detail about how local authorities might develop this work. The Practice Guidance on care management and assessment has appeared in three volumes, a Summary, a Practitioners' Guide, and a Managers' Guide. (The Summary is also included in the latter two volumes.) The rest of this chapter looks at aspects of assessment and care management, referring frequently to the Practice Guidance.

THE ASSESSMENT PROCESS

Once the local authority has decided to assess someone, it will have to go through several steps. These are described in the Practitioners' Guide:

deciding the level of assessment;

assessing needs;

deciding whether to arrange services to help meet these needs;

developing a care plan;

carrying out the care plan;

checking on – or monitoring – how things are going;

reviewing the assessment and the plan.

Deciding the level of assessment

The first step in the assessment process will be to determine the *level* of assessment, as distinct from the detail of the needs themselves. The Practitioners' Guide says that 'the assessment process should be as simple, speedy and informal as possible . . . based on the principle of what is the *least* that it is necessary to know to understand the needs being presented and to justify the investment of public resources' (para 3.3).

The Practitioners' Guide describes six levels of assessment which authorities might use, from 'simple' assessments for people requiring, say, a bus pass, which is available from a single agency under clearly defined rules; to a 'limited' assessment, again for a single need, but requiring consideration of certain criteria, say for low-level support at home; to a 'comprehensive' assessment, for severe, multiple needs and a high level of risk, requiring the co-operation of several agencies and services from different sources.

Assessors will need training in the initial stages of assessment so that they can identify the appropriate level. The Practitioners' Guide suggests that check-lists, or 'trigger' questions, will be useful in discovering if there is a deeper

FACTORS TO BE TAKEN INTO ACCOUNT IN A COMPREHENSIVE ASSESSMENT

The Practitioners' Guide (pp 58–59) suggests the following as a comprehensive assessment guideline:

Biographical details
Age, family circumstances, religion and ethnic origin.

Self-perceived needs

Self-care
How well the person can carry out basic tasks such as eating, dressing or bathing; how well they can get around.

Physical health
Checking whether a request for social care arises from a health need which could be improved.

Mental health
Checking to see whether a mental health need has developed unnoticed or unreported. The assessor will have to judge when it is appropriate to consult a health worker, such as the GP or a community psychiatric nurse.

Use of medicines
Checking to see if there are problems in taking essential medicines, and whether a pharmacist, GP or nurse should be involved.

Abilities, attitudes and lifestyle
Checking the person's situation in relation to their own expectations.

Race and culture
Appreciating racial and cultural diversity when identifying individual needs and how to deal with them.

Personal history
Making sure that the effects of past events – perhaps a bereavement – are fully taken into account in assessing present needs.

Needs of carers
Carers should always be aware of their entitlement to be involved and to be consulted (within the constraints of confidentiality). It should never be assumed that carers will have the same views about needs and care as

need than that which the person presents. One local authority is creating a new type of worker who will be responsible for finding out about the needs of people who approach social services, and for making sure that such people are put in touch with other relevant services and receive appropriate assessment.

Mr O'Malley lives close to local shops and a library. He has difficulty with the stairs in his maisonette. He contacts the social services department, which decides that his needs can be assessed by an occupational therapist.

the person being assessed – the assessor will have to weigh up the different views.

Social network and support
What other help is available, apart from the immediate carers?

Care services
What services are already being received, and how appropriate are they now?

Housing
Housing authorities and/or other providers (such as housing associations) should always be involved in the assessment if there may be a housing need.

Transport
Some needs may arise because of lack of suitable transport – for instance to get to the shops.

Risk
Different kinds of risk may be involved – for instance those caused by certain health conditions, such as diabetes or epilepsy; those caused by environmental hazards, such as the use of gas by people with dementing illnesses; or behavioural risks, such as threatening behaviour. The person being assessed may wish to accept certain risks which their families, perhaps, feel are unacceptable. Neighbours may be concerned about dangers with the use of gas. The assessor will have to weigh up these risks, with emphasis given to the person's entitlement to self-determination and independence (always bearing in mind that person's capacity to take informed decisions).

Finance
Assessors will be urged to make sure that the person being assessed and their carer(s) receive all the benefits to which they are entitled. Assessors will also have to test the means of the person being assessed, to see how much, if anything, they should pay towards the cost of care.

In the jargon of the Practitioners' Guide, this would probably be called a 'limited assessment'. It should be carried out by a qualified worker, but would involve only the social services department. In contrast:

Mr and Mrs Singh live in a first-floor council flat with no lift. Mrs Singh suffers from senile dementia; Mr Singh has a heart condition. Carrying groceries and helping his wife are becoming increasingly difficult. Their son lives ten miles away with his wife and three young children. They are able to offer support at weekends.

Mr and Mrs Singh have more complex problems. They need support for Mrs Singh – perhaps day care – and they really need rehousing. Mr Singh would like someone to sit with his wife once a week, while he attends the social evening at the local club. The assessment needs to take into account both their own circumstances and the contribution their family are willing and able to make to their care. They may need advice about benefits they could claim. Special attention should be paid to the needs of Mr Singh, as his wife's carer. He wants to go on caring for her, but if his health eventually breaks down this will not be possible.

This might be a specialist assessment – not quite as complicated as a 'complex' or a 'comprehensive' assessment, which are described in the Practitioners' Guide as being for high-risk situations, with severe or very complex needs.

Comprehensive – and other higher-level – assessments may involve many people in what is called multidisciplinary co-operation. Such work is often talked about, but it is not always easy to put into practice. Different professionals and other workers have varied backgrounds and training, and need to learn to build trust in the judgement of people from different disciplines in order to make their own distinct contribution, yet avoid overlapping or unnecessary duplication of work.

As we have already seen in Chapter 3, one aspect of community care planning will be to develop local agreements about joint working in assessment and care management, and in purchasing and providing services. The Managers' Guide discusses the important role to be played in assessment by GPs and their staff, community nurses, and therapy services. Government Guidance on training (*Training for Community Care. A joint approach*) shows how important a joint approach to training will be in helping workers and managers to learn to work together and to develop common values and skills.

Assessing needs

The assessments of Mr O'Malley and of Mr and Mrs Singh should ideally be carried out with their needs as they see them firmly in mind. It has been argued that in the past people have often been fitted to the services, rather than services made to meet the needs of the people.

The Summary of the Practice Guidance says that 'Care management makes the needs and wishes of users and carers central to the caring process. This needs-led approach aims to tailor services to individual requirements' (para 19).

However, the views of users and carers may differ: a carer may want regular breaks – periods of respite – whereas the person being cared for might not want to be looked after by anyone else. The Summary of the Practice Guidance states that if there is a significant problem, it may be appropriate to assess the carer's needs separately (para 39).

The Practitioners' Guide recommends that as far as possible users should participate actively in their own assessment – for instance by filling in their own assessment forms. However, some people are not able to express their views, or take an active part in the assessment. Their communication might be impaired through accident or mental disorder or they may not be able to speak English. Such people may need an *advocate* or *interpreter*, or access to a sign language or lip-reading service. Local authorities should give people information about local advocacy schemes if this seems appropriate; and the Guidance recommends that interpreters should be available if needed.

The Managers' Guide discusses different ways in which local authorities might make advocacy available to people who need it, suggesting that local authorities will wish to target their resources on users with a priority need, for example:

> users unable to express their own views who have no acceptable friend or relative to act on their behalf;
>
> users who are in dispute with the agency;
>
> users who have been previously disadvantaged, for example, minority ethnic users or disabled people. para 2.49

Especially for those users who are unable to request such assistance, there should be agreed criteria for triggering the involvement of advocacy support (para 2.50).

ADVOCACY

An advocate speaks *on behalf* of someone, as if they were speaking *for* that person. If the advocate knew the person before they became ill or disabled, they may well know what views the person would have. If not, the advocate will have to befriend the person, and try to find out by various means what the person would want for themselves.

Advocacy is important in representing the interests of people who are unable to make decisions for themselves, or who need support to have their say. *Self-advocacy* brings together groups of people to help them state their own views. *Citizen advocacy* provides trained ordinary citizens as advocates to represent the interests of people who need help in expressing their own views. People with learning disabilities and with mental health problems have historically had decisions made *for* them.

An advocate is not the same as an interpreter. An *interpreter* simply repeats what the person is saying.

The availability of advocates and interpreters is an important part of equal opportunities — ensuring that people are not disadvantaged by not being able to communicate with the people providing services or carrying out assessments.

If implemented, section 1 of the Disabled Persons Act 1986 would give local authorities the power to appoint an advocate for someone who cannot appoint his or her own representative because of any physical or mental incapacity, and section 2 would require the local authority to permit an authorised representative to act for a disabled person, at their request. However, these sections of the Act are *not* in force, even though they have been passed in law (see Appendix 1 for a further description of the Act).

Co-operation with health and housing authorities

The Act says that local authorities must inform the relevant authorities if people who ask them for assessment have health or housing needs.

Such communication will be essential, for instance, in the case of Mr and Mrs Singh. It is likely that they will need to find more suitable accommodation, perhaps in sheltered housing. They also have health needs which are likely to increase. The assessment process needs to take these into account at an early stage, so that any proposals for their care will have the full co-operation of all those involved. As we will see later, any 'package of care' which is devised for them must be agreed by all the agencies involved.

The local authority cannot assess someone as needing a nursing home place without agreement of the health authority. This will be an important area for clear definitions of responsibility, as we discuss on pages 139–140.

Confidentiality

Communication with other authorities and organisations should give due regard to the need for confidentiality. People need to know that their affairs will not be discussed without their permission. The Policy Guidance states that most communication between workers, such as between social workers and GPs, should take place informally – perhaps by telephone. Only in relatively complex cases should there be formal case conferences (para 3.35).

This makes it all the more important that people's privacy is protected, and that users of services know how local authorities and others will use and respect information about them. Some processes are now regulated by law. The Data Protection Act 1984, for example, is designed to make sure that computerised information relating to an individual is obtained fairly, kept up to date and stored securely. The person has a right of access to check the accuracy of the information. Confidentiality is protected by other Acts and Circulars which are listed in the Policy Guidance. These include the Access to Personal Files Act 1987 and the Access to Health Records Act 1990.

The Practitioners' Guide gives the following 'Principles of Confidentiality':

Information should be used only for the purposes for which it was given.

Information about a user/patient should normally be shared only with the consent of that person.

Information should be shared on a 'need to know' basis.

Users and carers should be advised why and with whom information concerning them has been shared.

All confidential information should be rigorously safeguarded.   para 1.21

Where will assessments be carried out?

Assessments will be carried out wherever is most appropriate. This could be in a person's home, including a care home, or in hospital after a fall or serious illness. Department of Health Circulars HC(89)5 and LAC(89)7 give guidance on the proper procedures to be carried out at the time of hospital discharge. At the time of writing it is not clear whether provision in these Circulars may be changed after April 1993. In any case, health and local authorities are required to show that they have agreed about how people will be assessed when they leave hospital, either to return to their current home or to move to somewhere more appropriate for their needs.

Assessing means

As part of the needs assessment, there will be an assessment of people's ability to pay for care services. A national system of charging procedures will be administered by local authorities for care arranged in a residential or nursing home; local authorities will each have their own system of charging for certain local social services. These systems are described more fully on pages 129–133.

Deciding whether to arrange services to meet needs

It is natural to assume that a 'needs-led' assessment means that the principle goal of the assessment is to meet needs as defined by the user. This is certainly indicated in the quotation from the Summary of the Practice Guidance on page 71, which states that the 'needs and wishes of users' should be 'central to the caring process', and refers to this as a 'needs-led approach'. However, the Policy Guidance shows that the responsibility for deciding which needs will be met lies firmly with the local authority. It says that in the assessment account will need to be taken of:

> the local authority's criteria for determining what services should be provided;
>
> the types of service they have decided to make available;
>
> the overall range of services provided by other agencies, including health authorities.   para 3.15

The Secretary of State for Health has stated that local authorities should 'carry out assessments of individuals with care, and ensure that they do not create commitments that are beyond their means'.[14]

What is 'need'?

The definition of 'need' depends to some extent on why it is being defined. People with apparently the same problem will say that they 'need' different kinds of help, depending on their own circumstances and preferences. 'Need' is sometimes defined differently from 'demand', which is the expressed preference of people who want services or help.

The Practitioners' Guide says that it is 'essential that all care agencies and practitioners share a common understanding of the term "need"' (para 10). In practice this may prove difficult, as the people and organisations involved may well have different aims and objectives.

The Summary of the Practice Guidance defines need as

> the shorthand for the requirements of individuals to enable them to achieve, maintain or restore an acceptable level of social independence or quality of life, as defined by the particular care agency or authority.   para 11

The Government's Guidance thus places the responsibility for defining the person's needs squarely on the assessor, not on the person involved. It further places the assessor's decisions in the context of the policies of the local authority where he or she works. It states that local authority council members must

> revise the policy framework within which managers and practitioners are asked to operate. A needs-led approach requires needs to be explicitly defined and prioritised in policy statements. Elected members ... have to ensure on a continuing basis that they are able to resource the response to the needs for which they accept any responsibility.   Summary, para 14

Local authorities are advised to publicise their definition of needs, making clear which they are *required* by law to meet, and those which the authority has *discretion* over:

> The more explicit the definition of need, the clearer users and carers will be about their access to services. By and large, local authorities have wider scope for interpreting their responsibilities in law in relation to the care of adults than to the care of children.   Summary, para 15

The Practice Guidance goes on to emphasise the *personal* nature of how people identify their own needs:

> Care management seeks to recognise the individuality of need by challenging practitioners to identify the unique characteristics of each individual's needs and to develop individualised, rather than stereotyped, responses to those needs within the constraints of local policy and resources.   Summary, para 17

> Ultimately, however, having weighed the views of all parties, including his/her own observation, the assessing practitioner is responsible for defining the user's needs.
> Practitioners' Guide, para 3.35

This appears to mean that in practice a 'needs-led' approach to assessment and provision of services may not be the same as a 'user-led' approach.

Fears have been expressed that assessments will be carried out with the local authority's definition of need in mind, rather than the user's. The situation is further complicated by the fact that *disabled people* must be offered a *comprehensive* assessment. The Practitioners' Guide states that the assessor will have to understand the 'local authority's interpretation of a disabled person' (para 2.20).

Thus there are no hard and fast rules. Different authorities are likely to define 'needs' and 'disabled person' in different ways.

A MATRIX OF NEED AND RISK

Berkshire Social Services Department's 1992 community care plan sets out a matrix for people in five client groups, describing different levels of need and risk, and putting them into priority order. Each of five major need categories (such as physical safety of the individual and others, or mental health of self or others) is related to a degree of risk to the user if the social services department does not meet some or all of the needs.

The primary need of the client will be identified, and its risk level assessed. The overall priority given to this combination will be the priority level for the client, and will determine what if any services can be arranged.

Priority 1 is allocated if there is high risk to the physical safety of the individual or carer, and intervention is needed immediately or within one week. Overall priority 3 is allocated to 'some risk of harm to the individual with actual evidence of harm — eg falls'. If 'opportunities for independent living/rehabilitation' is the primary need, overall priority 3 is given to 'very reduced quality of life. Severe loss of daily living skills or motivation/ confidence to use these skills.' Priority 5 is given to 'impoverished lifestyle due to limited daily living skills. Reduced independence.'

These are just some examples of how Berkshire is tackling the task of defining who will be eligible for services — *after* the assessment is carried out, in line with the Government's policy that arrangements for services should be targeted on those in greatest need, and within the limitation of available resources.

The care plan

The assessment procedure is part of the process of care management, which involves in addition the setting up and carrying out of a care plan, monitoring how it is working, and reviewing the assessment regularly. Where people have very complex needs, or need very high levels of services, their care may be arranged by 'care managers'.

There is no set pattern for how care management will be organised. In some authorities, the care manager will assess people's needs, help to work out a care plan, and monitor and review how the process is working, but they will not be responsible for managing budgets for services. In other areas, care managers will have special budgets for particular kinds of care. These are called 'devolved budgets' because they are moved away from the central administration of the authority. The idea is that the person who is closest to the service user will be able to make decisions about what kind of help is most appropriate, within the limits of that manager's budget. Such budgets are generally used to help people remain in their present home, and may be set at an amount per person somewhat below the cost of a place in a care home.

Mr O'Malley has tripped on the sill of the back door and fractured his hip. He is in hospital recovering, learning to walk with a frame, and contemplating returning home.

His family live 200 miles away. They are concerned that he might fall again and feel guilty that they can't visit more frequently. They feel he might be safer in a care home.

But Mr O'Malley is determined to remain at home, if necessary moving the bed downstairs. An assessment is arranged in the hospital, to sort out his care needs. The social worker, physiotherapist, occupational therapist and doctor all aggree on the services which will help him remain at home, and a care manager takes responsibility for arranging this support.

An arrangement is made with a neighbour to shop and do other errands for him. Mr O'Malley will contribute to the cost of this service. A home from hospital scheme will help with other care in the first few weeks. A physiotherapist and the home gardening service will also offer support.

From time to time Mr O'Malley's 'care package' will be reassessed. If his needs have changed or increased, he and the care manager may need to readjust it.

Mr O'Malley reassures his family that he would rather be at slight risk of another fall than move to a care home, away from his friends and neighbours.

Not everyone will have a 'care manager'. As they are gradually introduced, they will probably be used to support people with the most complicated needs. However the term care *management* (as distinct from care *manager*) simply describes the process of assessment and planning and review which should be part of all good practice. People without care managers should know who acts as their 'key worker' – the person who takes the major responsibility for their care, and who can serve as a link with other providers.

The care programme approach

There is a special 'care programme' approach for people who are patients of a consultant psychiatrist. This is described in Circular HC(90)23/LASSL(90)11. The aim is to ensure assessment and reassessment of people being treated in the community, and a formal discharge plan for every patient discharged from psychiatric hospital. Patients and their carers should be closely involved in preparing care programmes, which should involve the co-operation of various professionals such as nurses, psychologists, GPs and social workers. If a lack of resources prevents a patient's minimum needs for treatment being met in the community – in terms of both continuing health care and any necessary social care – inpatient treatment should be offered or continued. 'Health authorities will need to ensure that any reduction in the number of hospital beds does not outpace the development of alternative community services.'

The care programme approach is at the heart of one of the main aims of community care: the replacement of large, institutionalised hospitals with locally based care either in ordinary housing or in various forms of sheltered or supervised housing. The approach has not been adopted everywhere, although health authorities were due to do so by April 1991. There is concern in many areas that hospitals for people with mental illness are closing before adequate community facilities are available for people being discharged.

In 1992, the Government told health authorities that further closures of hospital facilities should not take place unless there was agreement with local authorities about alternative provision. However, some people feel the resettlement programme is being carried out far too slowly. There is a dilemma between the desire to move people out of large institutions into smaller homes and the fear that such a move may mean greater isolation, and perhaps neglect, if there are not enough resources in the community to provide appropriate support.

From April 1993 fundholding GPs will assume responsibility for a comprehensive mental health outpatient and community service. National Health Service Guidance (EL(92)48) states: 'where a fundholder purchases psychiatric services from an NHS unit or Trust, the contractual arrangement should require these organisations to operate fully the "Care Programme Approach"' (para 8.16).

DECISION-MAKING FOR MENTALLY INCAPACITATED PEOPLE

Many people who need community care services are not able to make decisions for themselves. They may have mental illnesses such as dementia, or learning disabilities, or have suffered brain damage through an accident or stroke.

We do not have a good framework for making decisions for such people. The National Assistance Act 1948 gives powers to detain people for their own or others' safety. Guardianship powers exist under the Mental Health Act 1983 for a guardian to make certain decisions about a person's welfare, but these are rarely used. Powers of attorney or receivership under the Court of Protection cover people's financial affairs but they do not cover personal decisions.

As part of the assessment and care management process, decisions will have to be made about whether people should be cared for at home or in a care home or hospital. Some people neglect themselves at home, yet are resistant to being helped.

Advocacy schemes as described on page 72 can help represent the views of mentally incapacitated people, but such schemes have no legal status and are not uniformly available. Sections of the Disabled Persons Act 1986 which formalise the role of advocates or representatives have not been implemented.

The Age Concern England book *The Law and Vulnerable Elderly People* looks at the many issues involved, as does a discussion report from the Law Commission *Mentally Incapacitated Adults and Decisionmaking: An overview*. Work is continuing to try to develop a way of making decisions for such people that fully protects their interests.

Reviewing the assessment

There may be differences of opinion about how the assessor defines or prioritises a person's needs. Part of the Disabled Persons Act which has not been implemented says that people should be able to have a *review* of their assessment under that Act. Some have argued that people should be able to appeal if they are not happy about the assessment and its outcome under the 1990 Act. However, the Policy Guidance states that:

> Decisions on service provision should be reached in discussion with users and carers and every effort should be made to ensure that the result is acceptable to them. A formal judicial appeal procedure would be foreign to such arrangements and it would not be appropriate to introduce one. para 3.54

The first step for people wishing to obtain a review of their community care assessment will thus be through the *complaints procedure*, which social services departments must now have (see Chapter 6). People must be told about this procedure when their needs are being assessed, but it remains to be seen how effective this will be in helping people to raise problems to do with the assessment process.

If, however, people feel that they are not being helped appropriately under the various relevant Acts, they can seek redress through the courts; they can also appeal to the Local Government Ombudsman if they feel the authority has not acted properly (see pp 106–107 for further details).

DILEMMAS OF ASSESSMENT

Assessment as rationing

Assessment should be a way of getting close to people's own views about what services they need. However, it can also be a way of weeding out people, to see whom the local authority will arrange services for, and who does not come high enough up the list. It is a way of 'rationing' services.

There is therefore a tension between the idea of 'user-led' assessment and the 'targeting' of resources on people in greatest need. Some social services departments are worried that the assessment process will raise expectations which cannot be met. It is possible that some assessments will not reflect people's *actual* needs, but only the needs they are allowed to express in line with those the authority feels able to meet. Such a system would suppress any understanding of the true level of need, unless the unmet needs are carefully recorded and fed back into the planning system.

In general, legislation about health and personal social services is interpreted as requiring authorities to do things *within the limits of available resources*. This is the broad framework within which the Government has based the community care changes. This means that it is difficult to define exactly how a particular need – or how many needs – should be met by public provision. Similarly, it is difficult for people to judge whether *their* authority arranges enough of a particular service or makes available a wide enough range of services.

The Acts of Parliament described earlier in this chapter create *duties* for local authorities, but they are rarely formally challenged over them. Frail and vulnerable people are often not in a position to press for their needs to be met when they are told that nothing is possible. It remains to be seen whether the new Act, and the new assessment procedures, will lead to formal challenges through the courts and judicial review when people believe that local authorities are not meeting their statutory duties. Chapter 6 discusses more fully how individuals can challenge local authorities where they feel their specific needs are not being met.

In addition to its rationing function, the assessment process may also be seen as a way of giving power to service users or potential users and their carers. If they are assessed as having needs which the authority then says it cannot meet, at least they then have knowledge which they can use to campaign for more or better services, or for more public funds to be spent on people with community care needs.

Acceptable risk

Assessment will reveal the difficulties of achieving a balance between allowing people to take risks and protecting individuals, their carers and other people. Professionals' views of 'acceptable' risk may not be the same as those of the individual, family or neighbours. Conflicts often arise, for instance, in judging what is 'acceptable' independence for someone who constantly leaves the gas on, thereby threatening the welfare of neighbours. The person concerned may refuse all assistance.

The use of the matrix described on page 76 will relate as much to the level of available resources as to any absolute judgement about reasonable levels of risk. Making public the criteria for allocation of priorities should once again empower service users, carers and other interested parties to raise the issue through the political process, if they feel that changes are needed to the system.

Judgements about risk are closely linked with 'choice' for service users.

Choice

The community care reforms are rooted in the idea that people should have choice about how their care needs are met. Assessment should be user-led, but gives the ultimate responsibility for defining need and working out how or if it will be met to the local authority through the assessor or care manager. How much choice the user will have will depend on many things, such as how much information the user has about available services; the resources the local authority has available; and the priorities that it has determined. For instance, it remains to be seen how much choice users will have to opt for residential care, when it lies well down the 'preferred options' for places of care. The amount of 'choice' available to a person needing to be protected through care, perhaps because they suffer from dementia, will depend on a fine balance in judging the amount of acceptable risk and the safety of the person or others.

It should also be remembered that 'choice' for users of community care may be severely restricted because of their illness or disability. In general, people have not 'chosen' to be in the position of requiring care, so frequently the choices available to them are options for improving a situation they would not have chosen. Many studies have shown that users of services often feel that they are given little or no choice when decisions are made about their care. The aim of the community care changes is that users and carers should be offered much more chance to have a real say in their care, but the assessors and all those who work in community care provision must learn to adapt to such a change.

Negative views of the assessment process

Assessment should be a positive process to find out as much as possible about a person's needs for care. However, if the assessment is seen as a hurdle to be got over, many people will be discouraged from approaching the authority for help. It may be quite difficult to overcome their diffidence, which might arise because:

— people may not understand how the procedure works;

— there may be no interpreting service to help people whose first language is not English, or who are deaf;

— people may not want their financial means to be assessed;

— disablement benefits have to be put towards services offered, when there is already difficulty making ends meet.

Careful monitoring will be needed to see how assessment procedures are working in practice.

Assessment and the process of care management will be used by the local authority within a framework of objectives and priorities to examine the needs of individuals, and then to decide which if any of these needs can be met by provision of services.

Assessment links with most of the other elements of the community care changes, particularly planning. Community care plans will set out the authority's priorities and may also show any gaps in service provision. The ideal is that the results of assessments of individual need should feed back into the planning process. Whether this ideal is met will depend on whether local authorities record the actual needs they find, or just those which they are prepared to meet. Reviews of assessments should also be important in showing how users feel about the services they are receiving.

Assessments will also link closely with the processes of purchasing and contracting, the subject of the next chapter.

5 Purchasing and Contracting

Until the community care reforms and the National Health Service review in 1989, most public health and social services were planned for and provided by public authorities. This was called 'direct service provision'. For instance, District Health Authorities operated hospitals and community health services. Social services departments ran their own residential homes – 'Part III homes' – and had their own home help services and day centres.

There were exceptions to this general rule. In some areas, voluntary organisations ran some services by arrangement with the local authority. For instance, the Women's Royal Voluntary Service has long provided meals on wheels on behalf of social services authorities. Many Age Concern organisations have been major providers of day care and other services. These would frequently have been run under formal arrangements and would have received financial help from the local authority in the form of a grant to help them provide the service.

LOCAL AUTHORITIES AS ENABLERS

The community care and health service reforms change the role of authorities which were previously mainly *providers* to that of *enablers*. As enablers, the local authorities will have a number of tasks which we talk about in this chapter. The Department of Health's Practice Guidance on purchasing and contracting describes the 'enabling' role of the local authority with respect to community care:

> to identify the needs for care among the population it serves, plan how best to meet those needs, set overall strategies, priorities and targets, commission and purchase as well as provide necessary services and ensure their quality and value.
>
> *Purchase of Service*, para 4.3

This role thus involves many of the planning activities which we looked at in Chapter 3. It also involves assessment and care management, as these are necessary if the local authority is to know what services it should purchase or provide.

The White Paper

The change to an 'enabling' role is said by the Government to offer more choice of services; to provide services which meet individual needs in a more flexible and innovative way; and to encourage competition between providers, resulting in better value for money and a more cost-effective service (*Caring for People*, para 3.4.3).

The White Paper also said:

> The Government will expect local authorities to make use wherever possible of services from voluntary, 'not for profit' and private providers insofar as this represents a cost effective care choice. Social services authorities will continue to play a valuable role in the provision of services, but in those cases where they are still the main or sole providers of services, they will be expected to take all reasonable steps to secure diversity of provision. para 3.4.1

Social services authorities still have to make sure that certain people have access to services if they need them: they have *statutory duties*, as we saw in Chapter 4 (p 45). But instead of providing most of these services themselves, the Government wants them increasingly to *arrange* services offered by a variety of *providers*. The providers can include the local authorities themselves, but also private, voluntary and other bodies. Authorities are thus encouraged to promote the development of independent sector provision – to develop what is called a 'mixed economy of care'.

This should not mean the end of 'council services'. The Government sees a continuing role for local authority direct provision, in particular for very dependent people or those with 'challenging behaviour', or where there are no other suitable forms of provision (*Caring for People*, para 3.4.11). It may mean, however, that some councils which are proud of the services they run will be encouraged by the Government to transfer some of these services to other providers, and to encourage independent provision in place of their own.

In the first year of the funding transfer, local authorities will be required to spend at least 85 per cent of the 'transfer element' of the Special Transitional

Grant (see pp 133–134) on community care services provided independently of the local authorities.

In their community care plans, local authorities will be expected to show how they will stimulate the independent sector to provide community care services:

> Social services authorities will be expected to make clear in their community care plans what steps they will be taking to make increased use of non-statutory service providers or, where such providers are not currently available, how they propose to stimulate such activity. *Caring for People*, para 3.4.5

They can do this by:

— devising specifications of service requirements and arrangements for tenders and contracts;

— stimulating the setting up of 'not for profit' agencies;

— identifying self-contained areas of their own work which can be 'floated off' as self-managing units;

— stimulating the development of new voluntary sector activity (*Caring for People*, para 3.4.6).

These suggestions have been taken up by local authorities in a variety of ways. Cornwall County Council has transferred three day centres, complete with staff and users, to the management of Age Concern Cornwall. Some authorities have helped new independent organisations with the cost of preparing business plans for taking over certain services. In addition, new money has been provided by the Government for local authorities to channel to independent sector providers to develop new community care schemes.

The 'purchaser–provider split'

The emphasis on purchasing and contracting and moves towards systems of assessment and care management have led many authorities to change their structures. They have divided tasks which were formerly carried out by the same people, or within the same section of the department. For instance, the home care organiser has traditionally been responsible for assessing people's needs *and* managing the service. In some authorities these responsibilities have now been split. One part of the department is responsible for assessing needs and arranging to *purchase* the necessary service from a *provider* – either another part of the department or an outside organisation.

Where this has meant reorganising a social services department into divisions or units with these separate responsibilities, it is often referred to as the 'purchaser–provider split'. Major changes in working patterns have already occurred in some local authorities. These changes will come about gradually, however, and will of course be differently organised in each authority.

Health authorities have already been required to make this change. They are responsible for assessing the needs of their local populations and purchasing services to meet these needs within available resources. Any directly provided services which they operate (and many are now run by separate NHS Trusts) *must* be separated from the purchasing responsibility. Interestingly, GP fundholders have increased purchasing responsibilities, but remain providers as well.

Some authorities have transferred services – particularly residential care – to specially created organisations. There are several types of 'not for profit' companies, or 'trusts', which have been developed to take on services, for example in Cheshire, Somerset and Tameside.

Tameside is a metropolitan borough near Manchester. It has transferred all its homes for elderly people to an independent organisation which is able to raise money on the open market to pay for improvements to the homes. Local authorities cannot freely raise money, as the amount they can raise for capital expenditure has to be approved each year by central government.

Because Tameside no longer has any homes of its own for elderly people, it is no longer a 'direct provider' of residential care. However, it still has a statutory duty under the National Assistance Act 1948 to provide residential care for people who need it and for whom it is not otherwise available. Tameside must therefore *arrange* places for older people as needed. It can do this either in its former homes or in other independent homes.

In doing this, Tameside will assess the residents' means to see how much they should pay for care, just as it would have done if the person lived in one of Tameside's homes before the transfer. From April 1993 it will use the new charging procedures described on pages 129–131.

In the jargon of the community care changes, Tameside is now a 'purchaser' of residential care: it arranges such care through contracts.

Arranging residential and nursing home care

The community care changes will extend local authorities' responsibility for arranging care by adding responsibility for arranging care for people needing continuing nursing care. The transfer of funds from the DSS budget to local authorities will particularly affect the purchasing and contracting responsibilities of local authorities, which will be responsible for arranging publicly funded residential care and social care for people at home, and much publicly funded nursing home care. The priorities they choose will determine the kinds of care which will be available for people whom they assess as having needs which they will support.

CONTRACTS

The Government has said that their bargaining power should enable local authorities to obtain good quality care from care homes or home care agencies at the most economic price – a principal goal of the community care changes. Contracts with outside organisations will be legally binding, whereas no such contract exists when services are purchased from provider units within the authority. Such internal arrangements are often referred to as 'service-level agreements'.

Types of contract

Some contracts will be 'block contracts': they will purchase a certain amount of services for a set amount of money. Others will be 'spot' contracts, or 'one-off' contracts. These will be individually designed to suit a particular person's needs.

A county in the south-west aims to have no block contracts for residential care. It hopes it will be able to allow substantial individual choice, developing a 'customised care plan' for each service user, and purchasing individual care home places as the need arises.

Contract specifications

Local authorities will be able to specify in a contract exactly what they want from a particular service. Kent County Council has set very detailed *service specifications* against which local organisations have been invited to tender for domiciliary care services. Contract (or service) specifications – and monitoring these – should be an important way of promoting quality.

According to the Government's Policy Guidance, users should be involved in drawing up service specifications. The views of users and carers should be taken into account. Local representative organisations, such as charities, may be important in speaking on behalf of people with different needs. Users' views of services will be fed back into the contracting process when the contract is due for renewal.

Service specifications will include details of the service, the quality and quantity of the service, and how these will be monitored. They will specify the length of the contract – for a particular period, or on a rolling basis, reviewed and extended, say, each year. (Independent providers mainly prefer longer contract periods so that they can plan their work over a longer time span.)

WHAT CONTRACTS SHOULD COVER

The Practice Guidance on contracting describes what contracts should cover, including:

— *the length of the contract (whether for a fixed period or renewable);*
— *what is being bought;*
— *how changes in the contract will be handled;*
— *the procedure for resolving disputes;*
— *default arrangements;*
— *insurance;*
— *complaints procedures for users and carers;*
— *the review procedure.*

The Practice Guidance says that social services departments should use race relations and equal opportunities laws to make sure that their contracting processes 'do not discriminate against women, people with disabilities or people from minority ethnic groups or their organisations' (*Purchase of Service*, paras 4.3.8–9).

A service specification can be a very long document. If a local authority has made a contract with a voluntary organisation like Age Concern to provide day care, both organisations want to be sure that they have covered all aspects of the service in the specification. After all, very large sums of money will be involved, and it is vitally important to make sure that the quality of the service is good.

Whom will the contracts be with?

In some areas of local government – for instance in refuse collection – local authorities have been required to put services out to tender, so that their own services and private services have had to compete to provide the service. In the case of social services, however, they are not *required* to do this.

Councils may put some services out to tender, or they may negotiate with private, voluntary or 'not for profit' organisations to see whether they would like to provide services under contract to the council. In general, the pattern of service provision will probably change only gradually, but here we discuss some issues of contracting with the voluntary and the private sectors.

Contracting with the voluntary sector

As we have already seen, some voluntary organisations have been providing services for many years. They have traditionally received grants from local authorities in recognition of the work they do, but not necessarily tied to a particular service or activity. There is now a move towards contracting – towards a 'contract culture', as it is sometimes described. Many local authorities are trying to distinguish between using grants for short-term work, or where small sums of money are involved, and introducing contracts for long-term funding or more substantial payments. Some authorities are linking agreement on contracts with continuation of general grants, a cause of some concern to voluntary organisations which do not wish to go down the 'contracting' road. Many local authorities have changed their attitude towards voluntary organisations whose services they may have grant-supported for many years.

A social services day centre organiser: 'In one area, we have a voluntary group which runs a well-managed, forward-looking day centre, which is putting in bathing facilities and can look after very dependent people. But we have to bring in people to my day centre from another part of the Borough, where the voluntary organisation has no intention of adapting to meet the needs of dependent elderly people. So, what do you do – remove their grant?'

This example illustrates a dilemma for some voluntary organisations which may not wish to change or expand their role, but which are dependent on local authority funding for some or all of their work. Although some voluntary organisations have been major service providers for years, others are now being encouraged to follow this route, funded through formal contracts or service agreements rather than by the less formal grant arrangements of previous years.

THE ROLES OF VOLUNTARY ORGANISATIONS

Sir Roy Griffiths summarised the varied roles of voluntary sector organisations:

self-help;

information provision;

befriending;

advocacy;

public education;

campaigning;

innovating and monitoring.   Griffiths Report, para 8.11

If voluntary organisations are increasingly expected to contribute to the 'mixed economy of care' by becoming service providers, there are some worries that their ability to act as independent observers of public policies and innovators of new types of care may be reduced. If they have a large contract with the local authority to provide one service, will they be able to comment on some other aspect of the local authority's policy without endangering the contract on which they depend? If they must follow the local authority's priorities in order to obtain a contract, they may have to neglect innovatory or less high priority schemes which may have been the main reason why they were set up in the first place.

There are other concerns about voluntary organisations and contracting. Contracting is a complicated process, involving legal responsibilities on both sides. Some small organisations will have neither the expertise nor the resources to deal with this. They are worried that they might be overlooked completely if authorities tend to turn to larger organisations to contract services, perhaps reducing or cutting altogether their grants to other organisations. This has already happened in some areas.

Most (but not all) services provided by voluntary organisations rely on volunteer help. Some concern has been expressed about the ability of such services to contract for tight specifications, when they depend on volunteers. The contract specifications may also require levels of training which volunteers do not wish to undertake.

These problems all relate to the nature of voluntary organisations themselves. Over the next few years it will be interesting to see whether the nature of these organisations changes even more than it already has as contracting increases.

Contracting with the private sector

Local authorities are also being encouraged to expand the range of services for which they contract through the private sector. Private care home provision has grown dramatically over the past decade, partly fuelled by the availability of special rates of income support. There is also a growing sector of private home care providers, although local authorities and some voluntary organisations have traditionally been the major source of help at home.

In some areas private sector providers believe that the local authority will be reluctant to contract with them. In other areas, reports show that private sector providers were not consulted over the preparation of the first community care plans, even though they were major providers of care. The Government's Social Services Inspectorate is charged with monitoring how well local authorities are encouraging the 'mixed economy of care', and, as we have seen, a legal obligation has been created for local authorities to consult with independent sector provider representatives in preparing community care plans.

The problem of uneven distribution of services – in some coastal areas, for example, there is an abundance of care homes, while in some inner cities or rural areas, there are few or none – sometimes results in service users having to travel long distances, perhaps to find an affordable place in a care home or, in rural areas, to reach a specialised day centre. Over time the aim of the mixed economy of care is that services should be attracted to areas where they have previously been underprovided. However, the transfer of DSS funds to local authorities in the early years will to some extent reinforce the unevenness in distribution of care homes (see pp 134–135).

The private sector is less well established as a provider of domiciliary care, and provides almost no day care. Most private domiciliary agencies are relatively small businesses, without the bargaining power of the well-established local authority services. Such agencies can often provide very flexible care, covering long or difficult hours at reasonable rates. They face similar problems to those of small voluntary organisations in coping with the often complex contracting procedures.

A brief look at contracting with the private and voluntary sectors may be in as much danger of overgeneralising as we are when we refer to members of 'client groups', as discussed in Chapter 1 (pp 19–22). Organisations and businesses in both sectors feel they have a lot to offer to community care, yet also wish to guard their individuality and special contribution to the overall pattern of care. Many are reliant on public funds and on their relationships with local authorities and – importantly – health authorities. In thinking about the 'mixed economy of care' it is important not to fall into the trap of thinking that all or even most of a particular 'sector' is the same.

Monitoring contracts

The Practice Guidance on purchasing describes a number of possibilities for monitoring how well contracts are working (*Purchase of Service*, para 5.6):

— The contract manager 'will monitor the quality of services offered as part of the contract management function'.

— In the case of residential care, the inspection unit may be asked to carry out evaluations of contract compliance, in addition to their statutory inspection duties.

— Care management staff will gather evidence and develop views about services, and receive feedback from service users.

— The formal complaints procedure and user satisfaction surveys will provide useful information; with vulnerable clients, 'the views of advocates should be sought'.

The Practice Guidance also says:

> Information systems must be capable of handling information on quality if it is to become a routine part of the management process. Most performance indicators relate to quantity and cost, thus providing a skewed view of services if taken on their own.   para 5.6.5

Monitoring is one of the most talked about parts of the community care changes, affecting nearly every aspect, but very difficult to do. There is a danger with contracts that they will specify items which are easy to quantify – such as number of staff and hours of care – but will have difficulty in identifying how *quality* can be checked on. In Chapter 7 we look in more detail at quality and standard-setting.

SOME IMPLICATIONS OF CONTRACTING FOR SERVICE USERS

Choice

We saw at the beginning of this chapter that the introduction of the 'mixed economy of care' and the 'purchaser–provider split' was meant to encourage more choice for users of services.

In practice, it will be important to see in each local authority how this works for service users. As part of their purchasing role, local authorities will be taking out contracts for provision of certain services – for instance, day care. Once such a contract is established for, say, three years, there may be little choice for service users if they are assessed as being able to benefit from day care, but there is only one place which provides it. If an authority places a block contract for home care services, will a user be able to use another home care agency?

For residential and nursing homes, the Government has placed a legal duty on local authorities to arrange a place in the home of a person's choice. This requirement is subject to certain conditions, for instance that the home can provide appropriate care to meet the assessed needs, and that the local authority does not have to spend more than it would in a home with which it would normally contract places. ('Top-ups' (see p 131) can be made if the fees are in excess of what the local authority would normally pay.) For day and domiciliary services, however, 'choice' will depend on the kinds of contract each local authority makes; and choice for people in residential care may in practice benefit only those who are able to arrange to pay extra fees or, indeed, who are able to express their own views.

Consumer power

When we enter into a contract, we have rights as consumers. We pay for a service or a product, and if that product is not fit for use or the service is not satisfactory, we are protected under consumer legislation on the sale of goods and services.

Consumers' rights with respect to contracted community care services will not work in quite the same way. In care homes, for instance, the local authority will be legally responsible for paying the fees. This means that the local authority purchases the place and pays the bill, and collects as much as it can from the resident. Thus the resident does not have a direct contractual relationship with the care home.

The same will be true for services provided in people's homes or in day centres. If the person is paying for the service directly, he or she can withdraw from the arrangement if the service is not satisfactory. If the person is using a service which has been purchased by the local authority on his or her behalf, the contract is then between the local authority and the provider – and possibly between the local authority and the user. The user does not have the power of the purse-strings to influence the service provider.

This means that the process of contract specification and monitoring will be very important to the user. If users' views cannot influence both the drawing up of specifications and the checking to see that these are met, the user's voice may be lost. The user will have very little purchasing power: it is always possible to end the arrangement, but since the user is dependent on the local authority for making the arrangement, and presumably cannot do without the service, his or her negotiating power may be very limited.

Some organisations of and for disabled people argue that the only way to give service users real choice and autonomy is to provide the money for them to purchase their own services. At the moment, the law does not give social services departments in England the power to do this, although it can be done in Scotland.

Tripartite contracts

This lack of personal power and other factors have led some people to suggest that there should be a 'tripartite contract' – that is, a contract between the service user and the local authority; between the local authority and the provider; and between the provider and the service user. Such a contract would set out the links between all three participants in the arrangement. In some cases, the service user would then be able to make some payment directly to the service provider, with the local authority paying the balance of the cost of the service. This would then give the service user direct power as a consumer and purchaser of the service. Some people sponsored by local authorities in charitable care homes have arrangements like this.

A provision in the NHS and Community Care Act (section 42(3)) amends the 1948 National Assistance Act (Section 26(3A)) to allow for such an arrangement if all those involved agree. This was seen as necessary for schemes funded by the Housing Corporation. The Government has stated that where this happens – or, in addition, where someone else is 'topping up' the fee – the local authority will continue to have ultimate liability for paying the full cost of the fees if either the resident or others involved do not pay the necessary amount (see p 131).

Even where there is not a formal tripartite arrangement, it is important that users should have full information about what they can expect from the service and what their obligations are.

Value for money and quality

Increased competition will result in better value for money only if the effect of the competition is to keep prices down without reducing quality. One way of monitoring contracts will be to look at the reports of the inspection units (see p 118). At first, most inspection units will be looking at residential care, and perhaps later evaluating other services which the local authority arranges or provides.

Fears have been expressed that the contracting process will force prices down at the expense of quality of care – perhaps resulting in a 'two-tier service', where people who can pay for their care get good quality care, while those needing support from public funds get a lower standard. It will be important for service users that monitoring ensures that services are of good quality, regardless of who is paying.

Quality of non-contracted community care services

At present, there is no formal registration or inspection system for care provided in people's own homes – domiciliary care. If a service is directly provided by the local authority and there are problems, the user can make a complaint through the complaints system; in future the inspection unit may check on such services. If the service is provided under contract by an outside agency – say a voluntary organisation or a private company – the local authority will also be able to check on the service through monitoring the contract. There will be no such protection (and indeed there never has been) for someone who simply buys in a similar service without involving the local authority. Some people believe that there should be inspection and registration of such services similar to that for residential care.

The purchasing and contracting process should have a number of advantages over previous arrangements for care services. These include the contract itself – a statement of what a service should provide, and how this will be monitored. Whether service users benefit from this process will depend on how much choice they are offered within the contracting system, and on how well checks for quality are made.

Other checks will also contribute to this process: complaints procedures and inspection units will be important elements in protecting the quality of services. These are discussed in the next two chapters.

D

6 Complaints Procedures

In local authority social services departments, complaints procedures are an important way of finding out how users feel about services. A complaint could be about the way a service is delivered, or the attitude of staff; about refusal of service; or about a delay in receiving a service. A complaint could also relate to failure to provide a particular service at all.

Complaints procedures are a process by which users can comment or complain, and staff and managers can respond. Complaints procedures are part of *quality assurance* – the way we keep track of how well services are doing. They help people offering services to learn from their experience, and to develop better services in the future. They offer service providers the chance to apologise and to make amends if things have gone wrong and to take steps to make sure that the problem does not arise again.

COMPLAINTS OR PROBLEMS?

Nobody likes complaints. When you think you are doing a good job, it is not very nice if someone says they do not like the way you do it. And people often feel guilty if they complain about services or help they are receiving – it somehow seems ungrateful. They do not want to be labelled as moaners, and they certainly do not want to lose the service, or risk bad treatment as a result of their complaint.

In a way, it is a pity that the procedure is labelled 'complaints'. Some examples of when people might need a complaints procedure will show that we are often talking more about 'problems' than 'complaints'.

Mrs Alberts attends a day centre three times a week. The people who attend the centre have got into the habit of sitting in the same place every day, which means that Mrs Alberts ends up sitting next to Mrs Thomas, who has great difficulty speaking because she has had a stroke.

Mrs Alberts would dearly love to have someone to chat with, perhaps on one day a week. She knows how important it is for Mrs Thomas to have a chance to talk, but she finds it frustrating not to be able to exchange news and views with someone else a bit more freely.

Mrs Alberts is not exactly sure how to tackle this. She doesn't want to appear to be a grumbler, and she certainly doesn't want to hurt Mrs Thomas' feelings.

In the language of the community care changes, Mrs Alberts should be able to express her views through the *complaints procedure*. It should be possible for her to sort out this problem through the *informal* part of the procedure, by having a quiet word with a member of staff, who should be able to respond sympathetically. If the staff member does not know how to sort it out, they should know who will be able to.

Some problems are more serious, and may need to be dealt with through the *formal* part of the complaints procedure.

Mrs Akram has had a home care worker three mornings a week for some time. Unfortunately, the worker has been ill, and several different workers appear to be filling in. None of them can speak Mrs Akram's own language, and she finds it difficult to understand what is happening. Her daughter has raised the matter with the home care organiser, who has said that nothing can be done. They are very short staffed, and her mother is lucky to have the service.

People like Mrs Akram and her daughter are often worried or confused about the service they are receiving, but they are not sure how to go about setting things right. They are often afraid that the service will be taken away if they complain. Sometimes it seems that anything is better than nothing. But is it? Mrs Akram's daughter may decide to take this problem a bit further – through the formal complaints procedure of the social services department. She will 'register' a formal complaint on behalf of her mother.

HOW A COMPLAINTS PROCEDURE SHOULD WORK

The White Paper and the Act

As already seen in Chapter 2, the White Paper (para 5.7) emphasised the importance of learning about the views of users and carers. It saw complaints procedures as one way in which this could be done (para 3.4.10). The NHS and Community Care Act confirmed this in law.

Section 50 of the 1990 Act amends section 7 of the Local Authority Social Services Act 1970. New sections inserted into the 1970 Act say that the Secretary of State for Health can by order require local authorities to

> establish a procedure for considering any representations (including any complaints) which are made to them by a qualifying individual, or anyone acting on his behalf, in relation to the discharge of, or any failure to discharge, any of their social services functions in respect of that individual. section 7B(1)

Someone is a 'qualifying individual' if '(a) the authority have a power or a duty to provide, or to secure the provision of, a service for him; and (b) his need or possible need for such a service has (by whatever means) come to the attention of the authority' (section 7B(2)).

The Complaints Procedure Directions were issued to local authorities in 1990, and printed as an Appendix in the Policy Guidance, which also gives fuller details of what is expected of local authorities in setting up complaints procedures. The Department of Health also issued Practice Guidance to local authorities (*The Right to Complain*), giving more detailed information about how local authorities might approach the complex task of making complaints procedures work.

Social services departments should have information easily available which tells people how to comment on or complain about services provided or arranged by them. A user of services might wish to use the complaints procedure or perhaps someone who has been told that nothing is available, but who believes that a service should be arranged for them.

Someone else can make a complaint on behalf of such a person – perhaps a relative or friend who can see that things are not going well. Carers might also wish to make a complaint, if they do not feel that their interests are being properly considered.

Essentials of a complaints procedure

There are certain things which must be part of every local authority's complaints procedure. These are described in the Policy Guidance, and are summarised in this chapter.

OBJECTIVES OF COMPLAINTS PROCEDURES

The Policy Guidance sets out objectives for complaints procedures. Complaints procedures should:

(i) provide an effective means of allowing service users or their representatives to complain about the quality or nature of social services;

(ii) ensure complaints are acted on;

(iii) aim to resolve complaints quickly and as close to the point of service delivery as is acceptable and appropriate;

(iv) give those denied a service an accepted means of challenging the decision made;

(v) provide in defined circumstances for the independent review of a complaint;

(vi) give managers and councillors an additional means of monitoring performance and the extent to which service objectives are being achieved. para 6.10

The Policy Guidance says that the starting point for complaints procedures is to protect the interests of individuals:

The spirit in which complaints procedures are implemented will largely determine their effectiveness . . . they are most likely to ensure quality and protect individuals when they stem from a recognition of users' needs and rights. They will fail to be effective if they are perceived by managers or staff as a threat. para 6.6

A report about complaints must be given each year to the social services committee. This is part of *quality control*. Complaints will be used as a way of checking on how services are doing, and to see where gaps may exist. Records of complaints should feed back into the planning process to see if new or different services are needed, or if additional staff training is required.

A complaints procedure should have three stages:

the informal or problem-solving stage;

the formal or registration stage;

the review stage.

The informal stage

If a person has a problem, the aim is to sort things out as quickly as possible, preferably where the problem arises. This will involve informal discussion between the user of the service and the staff. The user needs to know what the service is meant to offer, and how to make a comment or complaint if necessary. Staff and managers of the service have to be able to accept that a comment or criticism is not necessarily blaming them: it is a way of helping to make sure that the service is as good as possible.

The formal stage

If the complainant – the person complaining – is not happy with the result of the informal process, he or she may wish to register a formal complaint. This should be done in writing, and the complainant should be offered information about how to do it, and assistance if necessary. Complainants should be told how to find an *advocate* if necessary, to help to put their point of view (see p 72 for more about advocacy).

There should be one person – the *designated person* – in the social services department with special responsibility for the complaints procedure. This person is responsible for setting time limits for dealing with complaints, and for making sure that proper records are kept about complaints. The local authority will investigate the complaint and reply within 28 days, or tell the complainant why it has not. In any case, there must be a reply within three months.

The review stage

If the complainant is still not satisfied with the authority's response, he or she can have the complaint put before a *review panel*, which is described in the Directions and the Policy Guidance. There are three people on the review panel. At least one of these must be *independent* – someone who is not involved with the local authority. Such a person could be a member of a local voluntary organisation, for instance. Local authorities are encouraged to provide training for people who serve on review panels.

The review panel will investigate the complaint, perhaps interviewing the people involved, and must report in writing to the local authority and to the complainant within 28 days. Within 28 days of that, the local authority must give the complainant a decision in writing, stating the reasons for the decision and the action to be taken, if any.

The aim is to solve problems as quickly and as informally as possible. Hopefully it will not be necessary for many complaints to be made through the formal part of the procedure. Many users simply wish to be listened to and taken seriously.

COMPLAINTS PROCEDURES: A CHECKLIST

In order to be effective, a complaints procedure should have certain characteristics:

— *It should be acceptable to staff and users.*

— *It should be clear who is responsible for handling complaints.*

— *The procedure should be widely available and publicised.*

— *There should be an informal procedure — simple and quick, involving discussion and negotiation; a formal procedure — written, with a set timescale, and a report to the user; and some form of appeal or review.*

— *Advocates should be available to represent the interests of users who need such help. Interpreters should also be available.*

— *Confidentiality should be ensured.*

— *Complaints — both formal and informal — should be monitored and recorded.*

How the procedure might work in practice

Let us look again at Mrs Alberts (see p 99). If the day centre has a complaints procedure, it will have made sure that Mrs Alberts knows what services the day centre offers and how she can comment if she wishes to. She can speak to any worker at the day centre. The workers should all have had training in how to handle comments and complaints. If the worker does not feel able to deal with the problem, they should mention it to the person responsible for dealing with complaints. The organiser then has a quiet word with Mrs Alberts, and they work out together what is the best thing to do. They may perhaps talk about it generally with everyone who attends the day centre, and the staff, and arrange that one day a week people will sit together to share activities, rather than just social time. In this way, Mrs Alberts finds new companionship, but Mrs Thomas is not singled out as the cause of a problem.

A record is kept of the complaint, and the action taken. From time to time this record is checked, to make sure that the same kind of complaint is not coming up over and over again, or to see if some new kind of service or help is needed.

What about Mrs Akram? An informal approach to the home care organiser did not work. The authority has money problems. They are hard pushed just to arrange services for everyone who has been assessed as needing them. So Mrs Akram's daughter submits a written complaint, and goes with her mother to see the person responsible for complaints. The complaint is about how the service is being delivered, and also about the way the home care organiser responded to the initial complaint. Mrs Akram and her daughter would like an apology about this response, reassurance about how such approaches will be handled in future, and an appropriate home care service which recognises Mrs Akram's needs.

The complaints officer looks into the problem and finds that there is a local agency which provides care workers from different local ethnic communities. Everyone agrees how important it is for Mrs Akram to have appropriate services, and arrangements are made for the local authority to pay this agency to provide the care she needs.

The complaints officer makes a report of the complaint and how it was handled. He or she discusses it with the home care organiser, to try to sort out a better way of dealing with problems facing service users at a time of staff shortages. They decide to write to all their home care clients, explaining the problems they are facing and inviting anyone with problems to let them know. The record is fed back into the planning system. It is decided to find out just how many home care users have the same kind of problem as Mrs Akram. Perhaps next year a larger contract for home care services can be arranged with the agency.

They also prepare a leaflet describing the home care service in a number of languages, and make sure that it is widely available.

These examples show different kinds of complaints and complaints procedures. The law and the Guidance say that the social services department must have a formal, written complaints procedure. Other places will need complaints procedures as well.

What organisations should have a complaints procedure?

If users of community care services are really to be encouraged to have their say, there needs to be a complaints procedure wherever services are provided.

Other statutory bodies

Many community care services are provided or arranged by other authorities – for instance, the health authority or the housing authority. Where the local authority has arranged a service which is being provided under agreement by another authority as part of a 'care package', there should also be agreement about how a person can comment or complain, if necessary.

But some people will be using services without having come into contact with the local authority. Such services are still part of 'community care'. Each part of the health service, for instance, has its own system for dealing with complaints. The local Community Health Council should be able to advise users about these.

Non-statutory organisations

We have already seen that many non-statutory organisations – voluntary groups, housing associations, residential and nursing homes, home care agencies – will be providing community care services. Some of these services will be provided through a contract with the local authority, which is likely to require the service organisers to have a complaints procedure of their own. If the user is not satisfied with this, he or she can still use the formal local authority procedure.

Even when such services are not linked by contract to the social services department, it is a good idea for them to have a well thought out complaints procedure. This does not mean just handing a bit of paper to users – for instance, people in care homes – with a list of names saying what to do if there is a complaint. Too often we hear from people who say they do not dare to make a complaint, even though they know what they are supposed to do in theory. People must be encouraged to believe that it is all right to say how they feel, and staff need help in learning how to deal with comments and complaints. Otherwise, the whole exercise will be meaningless.

Complaints vs appeals?

As well as enabling users to say how they feel about services they are receiving, complaints procedures can also cover instances when services are *not* provided. This will probably be most important in relation to the assessment procedure which we discussed in Chapter 4.

If people who feel they need a service are not happy with the assessment, or with services offered as a result of the assessment, they must use the complaints procedure to have this reviewed. So although this chapter is mainly about service users saying how they feel about a service, it will also be relevant in situations where people feel they have been denied a service unreasonably, or wish to challenge the local authority about the services it is offering to them.

This means that the complaints procedure will be not only an important *problem-solving* process, but also an *appeal* process for the assessment system. Many people feel that it would be better to have a special review or appeal system for the assessment procedure, and leave the complaints system for services which are actually provided.

WHAT HAPPENS IF THE COMPLAINTS PROCEDURE FAILS?

Complaints procedures are one way for service users to make their voices heard. But what if things are still not right? Where else can people turn?

The Local Government Ombudsman

The Policy Guidance states that complaints procedures must include information about how to take a problem to the Local Government Ombudsman.

The Ombudsman exists to look into cases of what is called *maladministration* in local government. Maladministration occurs when a local authority has not carried out its work in a proper way.

It could be that a service user does not believe that the local authority has investigated a complaint or followed appropriate procedures in carrying out an assessment. If the service user or his or her representative wishes to make a complaint of maladministration against the local authority, they can contact the office of the Ombudsman, who will look into the matter and advise as to whether this could be a case of maladministration. If they judge that it might be, then an investigation will be carried out.

A complaint to the Ombudsman may result in the problem being sorted out after a relatively brief informal investigation. If more complex work is necessary, it can take up to a year, sometimes longer, to resolve. Either way, it is an important check on the way local government works, a way of ensuring that the proper processes are observed in providing public services. The address of where to write to find out about the Local Government Ombudsman is listed at the end of the book (p 161).

The courts

The courts may also be used to challenge the local authority about failure to provide a particular service. The NHS and Community Care Act lists the Acts under which community care services may – or must – be provided. These are described on page 64 and in Appendix 2. The Chronically Sick and Disabled Persons Act is described on pages 65–66. If people feel that they are not being offered a service which should be available under one of these Acts, they may be able to take an action through the courts.

It is possible to sue the local authority for breach of its statutory duty. This means, for instance, that it is not providing a service which it has a duty to arrange. It is also possible to seek a *judicial review*, a procedure through which the High Court supervises public bodies and makes sure that their actions are legal, rational and reasonable. A judicial review looks at what power or discretion has been given to the local authority, and whether this has been exceeded or misused. The court can set aside a local authority's decision, but cannot impose a decision of its own. Decisions under judicial review form case law which can be used in other cases.

People can also seek redress through the Secretary of State for Health, who can make an order to say that an authority is 'in default' if he or she 'is satisfied that any local authority have failed, without reasonable excuse, to comply with any of their duties which are social services functions' (section 7D of the Local Authority Social Services Act 1970, as amended by the 1990 NHS and Community Care Act, section 50). This is called a 'default power', and the Secretary of State can order the local authority to comply with a particular duty. Decisions by the Secretary of State under default powers are not made public. There is more about the various procedures in Age Concern's report, *Home Help and Care: Rights, charging and reality.*

ENCOURAGING PEOPLE TO MAKE COMPLAINTS

Even when everyone works hard to make sure that a service is as good as possible, there are times when problems come up which are not tackled. There are probably many reasons for this. One important barrier to an effective complaints procedure is diffidence about complaining.

When we use a service which is provided by 'experts' or 'professionals', or when we are very dependent on a service, we naturally feel nervous about expressing our feelings. We know that the 'expert' is very busy and we do not want to waste their time. We may be afraid that complaining will mean losing the service altogether. There is often a fear of retribution. Staff who work under great pressure, or for low pay, may also worry about their jobs, and react defensively when they feel criticised.

There may be a problem with communication: some people with community care needs may not be able to express their views, either because of their illness or condition, or because they do not speak English well enough.

Many people do not know what they ought to be able to expect from a service, and in any case they may not know how to complain. They may not believe that anything can or will be done to sort out the problem.

A complaints officer: 'Our complaints procedure is still in its infancy. Mainly we've had complaints about children's services under the Children Act. It's mainly relatives who complain about services for older people.'

Some service providers work very hard to take complaints procedures seriously, and to encourage users to express their views. One way of doing this is for local authorities to check on all services, to find out how easy it is for people to make comments or complaints. Staff can be trained and encouraged to look around, and take note when they observe things which might not be quite right.

Others may discourage comments, in the belief that 'we are doing a good job' or 'doing the best we can'. 'People come so there can't be any problems – we're full' is often used as evidence of a good service, despite the fact that no other similar service may be available.

In general, people who do complain – or express their views – frequently find that this *does* improve things. Perhaps a member of staff really has been mistreating someone; perhaps the food really is not adequate. Complaining is difficult, but if no complaint is made, then the bad practice is certain to continue. Sometimes responding to a comment or complaint will mean explaining honestly why a particular thing *cannot* be done. Trying to protect people from the truth about lack of money or resources can seem to them like being fobbed off with no information at all.

Making complaints can also be a problem for staff who see bad practice, but who fear for their jobs if they complain. Talking to someone in confidence outside the place of work may help to get the problem looked into and put right. However, 'whistle-blowing' often leads to the loss of a job. It is not easy to do. At the time of writing, the Government plans to issue guidance on 'whistle-blowing' in the NHS.

Advocacy and complaints

Some people will need an *advocate* (see p 72). They may not be able to express their own views, perhaps because they cannot speak after a stroke, or because they suffer from dementia. The Government's Directions to local authorities on complaints procedures state that they must offer 'assistance and guidance' to the complainant or give advice on where it can be obtained. Some local organisations may have specially trained people who can act as advocates.

The Practice Guidance on complaints procedures recommends that social services departments should consider keeping a register of agencies and individuals that might provide help and support to clients.

Confidentiality and complaints

People will want to make sure that their complaint will be treated confidentially. No one likes to have their problems talked about by others. When people are frail or vulnerable, it is particularly important that their right to dignity and privacy is respected at all times. Respecting confidentiality is one important way of doing this.

The Practice Guidance sets out principles of confidentiality:

> that information should only be used for the purpose intended;
>
> that information should normally be shared with the consent of the individual user/carer;
>
> that information should only be shared between agencies on a "need to know" basis.
> *The Right to Complain*, para 6.30

The need for confidentiality when dealing with complaints will be an important part of *training* for all staff and helpers.

Overcoming the influence of ageism

Another barrier to an effective complaints procedure is the influence of 'ageism' – having negative or preconceived images about what older people will be like *just because they are old*. In general, our society attaches glamour to being young. Many people fear growing old and becoming dependent. Popular fashion and music all focus on slim, trim images of youth. Birthday cards joke about each additional year – 'over the hill' at 40, for instance. Sports broadcasters call competitors 'geriatric' when they are in their 30s. Doctors advise older people to 'learn to live' with aches and pains, often asking 'What do you expect at your age?'

It is certainly true that as we grow older, we can expect changes. Ageing is a gradual process which takes place throughout our lives, but growing older is *not* a time of inevitable dependency.

If people working in community care expect old age to be a time of decline, they will not see the full potential of the help they can offer nor will they expect older people to say how *they* feel about the services they need. They will see an 'elderly person' instead of a 'person' who has his or her own history, desires and wishes. They may offer a service they think is 'best', but which does not meet the needs of that particular person.

Ageism also affects the expectations of service users themselves. Older people are often reluctant to 'bother' anyone about their problems. They may not be aware of what can be achieved. They may need help to believe that their situation can be improved.

Racism and sexism also impose preconceived stereotypes which intrude on people's individuality and expression of their needs. If meaningful complaints procedures are to be set up, all such attitudes will have to be challenged.

There is much talk these days about 'charters'. A good complaints procedure is not a 'moaner's charter'. Nobody has the right to complain just for the sake of it. But it should be the foundation of a 'user's charter' which encourages users of services to have their say and helps everyone involved to see services as belonging to the users and meeting their needs.

7 Inspection

Like 'complaints', the word 'inspection' can create negative images. It sounds like something that is 'done to' people or services – and, of course, in one sense it is. However, inspection can and should be much more than that. It should be one of the many ways in which we help improve the *quality* of all care services.

From April 1991, local authority social services departments have been required to have 'inspection units'. Local authorities are responsible for *registration* of private and voluntary residential homes, and for *inspection* of all residential homes in the area, including those run by the social services department itself. In future, the inspection units may check on day care or home-based services arranged or provided by the local authority, but they are not required to do so. The units also have responsibilities under the Children Act 1989.

WHAT IS AN INSPECTION UNIT?

The White Paper *Caring for People* said that local authorities should set up independent inspection units to inspect and report on both local authority and registerable independent residential homes. Local authorities already had a duty to register and inspect *independent* homes, but they did not have to inspect their own homes. This sometimes meant that local authorities set standards for private and voluntary residential homes which were not met in their own homes.

Section 48 of the NHS and Community Care Act 1990 gave new duties to local authorities to inspect their own homes. To make sure that they do this fairly –

or even-handedly – the inspection units have to be set up so that they are 'independent of the day to day management of local authority homes' (*Caring for People*, para 5.19). The units have to be responsible to the Director of Social Services but they are meant to be separate from direct management of homes, or other services which they may eventually inspect. This has led to the units being referred to as at 'arms-length' from the direct provision of social services. (At the time of writing, the Government proposes that from autumn 1993, units should report to the authority's Chief Executive.)

What do these units do?

As with everything to do with community care, the way the units are set up and their exact tasks will be different in each local authority. Some authorities have brought complaints, registration and inspection, and standard-setting into a unit which might be called 'Quality Assurance', or 'Quality and Standards'.

Much of the work of inspection units with residential homes will be based on requirements set out in the Registered Homes Act 1984 and Regulations related to this Act. The inspection unit's tasks will include:

— registration of private and voluntary residential homes. This task does *not* include registration of nursing homes, which is carried out by the registration officer of the District Health Authority;

— inspection of all registered residential homes in the area with four or more residents;

— working with residential home proprietors to improve the quality of care;

— setting standards which homes will be expected to meet;

— making publicly available reports to the social services committee about individual inspections, and about the work of the unit in general;

— working with an advisory committee and seeking the views of users of care and their relatives or representatives;

— using their work to feed back into the planning and purchasing and contracting systems.

REGISTERING RESIDENTIAL HOMES

Mr and Mrs Anderson live in a large house with several spare rooms. The couple have always enjoyed the company of older people, and Mrs Anderson worked for many years as a state enrolled nurse. For several years, they have cared for two older people, treating them as part of the family. Because they cared for fewer than four people, they did not have to register as a residential home. Nor did they have to be inspected as a residential home by the local authority.

However, a new Act of Parliament (the Registered Homes (Amendment) Act 1991) provides that from April 1993, people who run 'small homes' must be registered under a simplified procedure. Instead of doing this, Mr and Mrs Anderson have decided to devote more time and resources to helping dependent people to live a fulfilling life. They want to build an extension to their home, and become fully registered.

Mr and Mrs Anderson will have to give a lot of thought to this venture. Their first step will probably be to contact the inspection unit of the local authority, to find out what they will have to do in order to be registered to run a residential home.

If Mr and Mrs Anderson decide to run a residential home for four or more people, they will have to be registered under the provisions of the Registered Homes Act 1984. One part of the inspection unit will be responsible for registering homes.

Registerable homes

A 'registerable home' under the Act is one that provides 'board and personal care' for four or more people who need such care 'by reason of age, disablement, past or present dependence on alcohol or drugs or past or present mental disorder'. The care provided is said in Government Circular LAC(77)13 to be similar to that which a competent and caring relative could provide at home. Residential homes are not allowed to provide 'nursing' care, although such care can be brought in for a resident.

As we have already mentioned, small residential homes for three or fewer people are required from 1 April 1993 to register under a much simpler procedure.

Certain homes do not have to be registered: they are 'exempt'. These include homes provided by any organisation constituted by Act of Parliament (this includes homes run by the local authority) and homes run by an organisation incorporated by Royal Charter.

Requirements for registration

Requirements for registration of residential homes for four or more people are contained in the Registered Homes Act 1984 and in the Residential Care Homes Regulations 1984. The local authority has to be sure:

— that the applicant for registration or any other person concerned with running the home is a 'fit person' to be involved with a residential home;

— that the premises are 'suitable' for the purpose of the home;

— that the way it is intended to run the home will provide the services or facilities reasonably required.

It is important to remember that the home itself is not what is registered but the person (or persons) responsible for running the home (the owner, and/or the manager).

The law does not define a 'fit person', or 'suitable premises'. Each local authority therefore interprets the rules in its own way. Many authorities use *Home Life* in deciding how to interpret these terms. This is a code of practice for residential care which was endorsed by the Government as having similar status to Guidance. However, this book was published in 1984 and it is generally agreed that it needs revision.

Once a home is registered, it must display a registration certificate showing the name of the person registered; the total number of residents for whom both board and personal care are to be provided; and the age, sex and category of people who may be cared for.

Each local authority interprets the requirements of the Regulations in its own way. Thus neighbouring authorities may have different requirements for residential homes. For instance, many authorities have restrictions on the size of home they will allow, although there is no 'ideal' size for a home. If a proprietor believes that the authority is interpreting the Regulations unfairly, he or she can take the matter to a Registered Homes Tribunal.

Many people believe that there should be national standards or guidelines which homes in all areas should have to conform to. Some national organisations operate homes in different parts of the country. They find themselves having to work to different standards set by the various health and local authorities.

Concern also arises because neither the law nor the Regulations require homes to have written contracts with residents, setting out what they can expect to receive from the home in return for their obligation to pay the fees. At present, the home's obligation to provide a contract can be fulfilled by statements about the home's facilities in the brochure. A formal contract between the resident and the home is particularly important where people are not supported by the local authority. Some inspection units recommend that all homes have contracts with residents as a matter of good practice, although such contracts vary in content enormously.

THE FACILITIES AND SERVICES RESIDENTIAL HOMES MUST PROVIDE

According to the Regulations, the person registered must run the home so as 'to make proper provision for the welfare, care and, where appropriate, treatment and supervision of all residents'.

Section 9 of the Regulations describes the facilities and services to be provided, considering the size of home and the number, age, sex and condition of residents. These include:

— *employment by day and, where necessary, by night of enough suitably qualified and competent staff to be adequate for the well being of residents;*

— *'reasonable' day and night-time accommodation and space for residents;*

— *adequate and suitable furniture, bedding, curtains and floor covering, and, where necessary, equipment and screens in rooms occupied or used by residents;*

— *the adaptations and facilities necessary for physically handicapped residents;*

— *adequate light, heating and ventilation in all parts of the home occupied or used by residents;*

— *maintenance of all parts of the home occupied or used by residents in good structural repair, clean and reasonably decorated;*

— *regular laundering of linen and clothing;*

— *arrangements where necessary for residents to receive medical and dental services;*

— *suitable arrangements for recording, safekeeping, handling and disposal of drugs;*

— *suitable arrangements for the training, occupation and recreation of residents.*

There should also be facilities for visits to residents — in private if people wish. The timing and other arrangements for visiting can be decided by the person registered, in consultation with the registration authority.

Every resident should be told in writing how to make a complaint, and the person registered must make sure that any complaint is fully investigated.

INSPECTING RESIDENTIAL HOMES

Once the registration section of the inspection unit has completed the registration process for an independent home, the law requires that the home be inspected at least twice a year. Since 1991 local authorities have had to ensure an 'even-handed' approach between these inspection procedures and those which they have introduced for their own homes. The Government's Policy Guidance suggests that they bring about consistency of approach by the application of their local guidelines on registration to residential homes in all sectors, as well as the provisions of the Residential Care Homes Regulations (where appropriate) and of *Home Life*. The frequency of inspection should be 'a matter of judgement in each case, subject to statutory requirements where they apply' (paras 5.27–28).

What is inspection?

Inspection is a process of evaluation. It considers various things which, taken together, contribute to the *quality* of the service. The Department of Health's Practice Guidance on inspection, *Inspecting for Quality*, says that this evaluation of a service or set of services should include:

the resources devoted to the provision of the service;

the processes involved in providing the service;

the quality and quantity of service provision;

the quality of life of users.   para 4.1

The purposes of inspection are to help ensure that:

the quality of life of users meets agreed standards and that individual users and staff are protected from abuse, neglect or exploitation;

statutory needs are met and good practice is promoted;

action is identified to improve performance against established standards;

policies exist to make sure that staff recruitment and training support service development;

services are cost effective.   para 4.5

What happens during an inspection?

A formal inspection usually lasts a day or longer. The inspectors will check to make sure the registration details are correct (where appropriate), and on the number of residents and their well-being. They will look at the home itself, to see that it is in good condition, and to see whether repairs or maintenance are needed. They will check on staffing numbers and training, and see that essential records are being kept properly. They will try to look at all aspects of the home.

Less formal inspections will be more frequent. At least one inspection a year should be unannounced. Inspectors can arrive at the home at any time, and may check more informally on how residents feel about living in the home.

The inspection unit will prepare reports of individual inspections, which should be publicly available. In addition, it will be required to prepare an annual report on its inspection work. This report should be publicly available, and should identify homes unless there is a legal reason why it should not do so.

At the time of writing, the Government proposes that from autumn 1993 reports of individual homes should show what is good and what needs improvement. Reports should contain a jargon-free summary of findings, and the Social Services Committee should say publicly whether or not findings are accepted, and how they will be acted on. From autumn 1993 the Government also proposes that at least one lay person – an 'independent assessor' – should be part of every inspection team.

In some authorities, the inspection unit does more than the minimum. One authority carries out four inspections a year. 'Our standards are high – extra money was invested in our unit *before* the cuts.'

But some authorities do not even do the minimum. In some areas, there are simply not enough inspectors to inspect all homes twice a year. In other areas, the inspection unit may focus on homes where there are known to be problems, perhaps inspecting these more often than twice a year, and seeing the 'good' homes at less frequent intervals.

Standards of care

Doubts remain as to whether two inspections a year provide enough outside monitoring of the quality of care.

A social services department's residential care organiser: 'I don't know that two visits a year are adequate. We monitor our own homes every week or every other week . . . if we were to use the private sector more, the social worker would need to see the residents more – people would need ongoing social work or advocacy.'

It is possible for poor practice to go unchecked in homes in any sector. It may be difficult to pick up the fact that staff do not treat residents with sufficient courtesy or dignity, or that the regime of a home requires residents all to be in bed, say, by 8 pm, or that the food is inadequate.

These and similar problems do not necessarily arise through malice. By and large, the problems which arise in running homes occur for other reasons. These can include shortages of staff or funds; poor staff training; a lack of understanding on the part of the home's proprietors of the needs of residents; or frustration felt by staff because of the difficult behaviour of residents or pressure from families who may themselves be feeling guilty because they could not continue caring for their older relative.

THE IMPORTANCE OF BASIC VALUES

The inspection unit is helped in its work by a number of publications from the Social Services Inspectorate of the Department of Health. These include a workbook for inspection called *Homes are for Living In*, which stresses the importance of basic values which contribute to the quality of life of residents. These are:

Privacy
The right of individuals to be left alone or undisturbed and free from intrusion . . .

Dignity
Recognition of the intrinsic value of people regardless of circumstances by respecting their uniqueness and their personal needs . . .

Independence
Opportunities to act and think without reference to another person, including willingness to incur a degree of calculated risk.

Choice
Opportunity to select independently from a range of options.

Rights
The maintenance of all entitlements associated with citizenship.

Fulfilment
The realisation of personal aspirations and abilities in all aspects of daily life.   *Homes are for Living In*, p 16

Where any of these ideals needs to be restricted – for instance in making decisions for people who cannot make them for themselves – the reasons for limitations should be stated and the restrictions regularly reviewed.

At the same time as ensuring that statutory requirements are met, the inspection unit works with homes to improve standards of care. There are any number of ways in which this may be done. The inspection unit may advise on staff training; on equipment or alterations which would help the home provide better care; on attitudes on the part of staff or managers to residents and their relatives; on coping with difficult situations which may arise.

The unit will include in its report of an inspection recommendations for ongoing work to improve standards. Such work is endless: no care is ever 'perfect', so even a home offering very high quality care will have room for improvement somewhere. The inspection process should help to avoid complacency.

Inspection may sometimes uncover things which are totally unacceptable, such as abuse, unwarranted restraint, or too few staff for the number of residents. If the situation is bad enough, the inspection unit may serve notice that if changes are not carried out, they will take steps to close the home. This is of course a serious move, and one which is not taken lightly. It is extremely disruptive to residents to find that their home is to be closed and that they must move. Such a decision may be disputed by the home, which will have the right to take the decision to a Registered Homes Tribunal, which will look at both sides of the argument and decide whether the home should be closed.

As with complaints, there is a dilemma about how far to go in tackling bad practice which is not an infringement of relevant laws. One inspector believes it should be brought into the open: 'We shouldn't be taking responsibility for covering up deficiencies.' The charity Counsel and Care has published two relevant reports on aspects of care in homes: *What if they hurt themselves?* and *Not such private places*.

Physical standards

Inspection aims to promote high quality care, and inspectors look not only at standards of care in the home but also at physical standards.

There is a paradox in the inspection task. Good practice in residential homes emphasises the need for 'homely' surroundings. Yet some requirements for homes, which inspectors and others responsible must insist on, can be anything but 'homely'. Homes have to conform not only to the requirements of the inspection unit, but also to those of the Fire Safety Officer and the Environmental Health Department.

Most such requirements are laid down for the protection of people living in communal homes, where hygiene and fire safety may be of paramount importance. But for people in wheelchairs, negotiating fire doors can be difficult, if not impossible; and food safety regulations may prevent residents from participating in a 'homely' way in preparation of food. There is more work to be done on how to create a homely environment which is safe for those who live in it.

Many local authority homes are quite old, and their physical standards often fall short of those required of private and voluntary homes, although standards of care may be very good. In some areas authorities have decided to close homes or to transfer them to independent providers, rather than spend, from already overstretched budgets, the large sums of money needed to bring them up to standard. In other areas authorities will work over a period of years to bring the physical standards of their own homes into line with those of independent homes.

An inspector: 'We have to accept that some standards can't be met immediately — we have constantly to be working towards them.'

Many inspection units are preparing their own material about standards of care for home owners and managers in their areas.

INSPECTING NURSING HOMES

We have seen that local authorities have powers to inspect only residential homes. From April 1993, however, they will be purchasing places for people assessed as needing them in nursing homes.

Nursing homes are registered and inspected by the District Health Authority under separate regulations from those for residential homes. In debate during the passage of the NHS and Community Care Act, the Government was urged by many people to combine the inspection and registration system for both types of home. The argument was that it is difficult to assign people neatly into a 'nursing' or 'residential' category: elderly people, in particular, often have needs which can fall between the two. A category of 'dual registration' does in fact exist, whereby homes are registered both as nursing homes and as residential homes. This means that if a resident develops extensive nursing needs, he or she should not have to move to another home to find suitable care. But it also means that the home has to be registered and inspected by both authorities, which can be quite a complex process.

The separate systems were not altered by the Act, so health authorities remain responsible for the inspection and registration of nursing homes with which local authorities may be placing contracts for care. This means that the two authorities will have to agree on how the local authority will have access to such homes for the purpose of monitoring how its contract specifications are being met.

Some authorities are overcoming the problem by developing joint inspection units, combining health and local authority inspection staff, and developing joint working (see p 57), with each continuing to be responsible for its respective statutory obligations.

Nursing in residential homes

The blurred boundaries between 'health' and 'social' care which we discussed on pages 58–59 are evident in many residential homes, which strictly speaking should not provide nursing care. Such homes may *bring in* nursing care, but should not themselves offer it. Yet many residents in residential homes become increasingly frail and require nursing support. Such people are often very happy in the residential home, and managers who are qualified nurses may offer nursing care – against the rules, unless under the authority of a district nurse. In addition, it is sometimes said that unqualified care staff also carry out what are technically nursing duties. This may mean that residents of such homes are dependent for health care on unqualified personnel, with little protection if things go wrong.

Dual registration is one way round such problems, but it is not always appropriate, particularly for small homes for whom it may be too expensive and complicated. The increasing dependency of people in residential homes adds strength to the arguments of those who believe that the distinction between residential and nursing homes should be abolished.

INSPECTING NON-RESIDENTIAL SERVICES

At the time of writing, there is little provision for the inspection of day care services or services provided in people's own homes. There is no legislation to regulate such services.

Under the community care changes, there will be ways in which users of such services may be protected – through the assessment process, through the monitoring of contracts, and through the complaints system. In this way the changes should provide new ways in which users of *contracted* services can make their views known. It is also envisaged that in future inspection units should include in their work day and domiciliary services provided or arranged by local authorities.

Such protection will not apply, however, to people who purchase services for themselves. The United Kingdom Home Care Association (UKHCA) – an association of independent home care services – has developed its own set of standards to help ensure high quality care for service users. The Joint Advisory Group of Domiciliary Care Associations has published a document on standards for domiciliary care to encourage local authorities to extend their 'arms-length' inspection and regulation work to agencies which provide domiciliary care. But observance of such standards is at present voluntary, although some local authorities are introducing voluntary registration procedures. Many people argue that there is a need for better regulation of such services and increased protection for people using them. Similar concerns arise with day care services.

SETTING STANDARDS

In carrying out its inspection work, the unit will be working to standards which it has prepared, and which should be publicly available. In this way, home owners and managers, staff, residents and their families or representatives will all know what to expect of care in a home. The inspection process should thus be based on explicit values and measurable standards.

The inspection process is part of *quality control*, the process of testing how well a service is doing against standards or specifications which have been set for it. In setting out standards of care and then testing how well they are being met, inspection units will be checking on quality on behalf of service users. The inspection process is thus one way of protecting service users, although it should not substitute for other ways of helping users to express their views.

Setting standards is not an easy process. Ideally it will involve local experts, service users, central government, service providers and politicians as well as members of the inspection unit. Standards will be built around a framework of values which express the philosophy on which the service is based.

Important values in community care services are the belief in the fundamental dignity and worth of each user of services, and the importance of equal opportunities in providing services and letting people know about them. The activities and process of inspection, the Government's Practice Guidance says, should be anti-discriminatory and ensure that there is equal access to community care services irrespective of the race, culture, religion, gender, age or disability of the user.

DEVELOPING BETTER RELATIONSHIPS

The Relatives Association has been formed to bring together relatives of people in all types of care home, to help them develop better relationships with care home proprietors and staff, and to tackle some of the areas of bad practice which persist, despite all the attempts to protect the interests of residents.

Standards will also be based in part on work done by the Social Services Inspectorate of the Department of Health, and on *Home Life*.

Training and maintaining standards

Training is an important aspect of promoting standards in care. It is important both for people directly providing services and for their managers. In recent years there has been an important development in training for people at their place of work. National Vocational Qualifications (NVQs) have been developed for people who work in residential, day and domiciliary care (as well as in many other fields). Increasingly, their use may come to be seen as part of the standards which are set for service providers. This should benefit workers and service users alike, creating increased job satisfaction and promoting better quality care.

STANDARDS[15]

A standard is a yardstick

It is a way of judging how well a service is doing. It is a statement which should be able to stand up to measurement and be acceptable both to the people who must keep to it and to the people who will be served by it.

Standards for services can relate to many different aspects of a service. These can include:

the law or regulations; values; rules and guidelines of the organisation (or of government); codes of practice for particular types of service, or professional standards.

Standards should be *precise statements* which can be measured and which can work in practice. Some standards should be achievable immediately; others can represent aims to be worked towards.

Standards can be measured or tested in different ways. Some will relate to the number of people providing a particular service for a certain number of users. Others will relate to the quality of life as experienced by users. Some will be *objective* (they can be measured or quantified); others will be *subjective* (they will be about how people feel, or how satisfied they are). They may be about buildings or equipment or numbers of staff, or about attitudes and general approach.

Standards must be based on basic principles or values of service. They need to relate to what is put into a service to achieve the aims of that service and what is achieved – the outcome.

The role of users in setting standards

The views of users are particularly important for setting standards, as it is easy to develop standards which relate mainly to professional values, or the values of providers. These may not always reflect the views of users.

However, as we have seen, many service users and their carers are not used to having their say. They often feel guilty about complaining or commenting, and are sometimes afraid that the service will be taken away if they say how they feel.

An inspector: 'It's a black hole in the inspection process – getting comments from residents or relatives . . . we don't get relatives or residents queuing up to see us because they don't know we're visiting . . . there's an unconscious fear about making a fuss. So we're actively looking at ways to get round that – we'll be posting signs a month in advance of inspections, inviting residents and relatives to put their point of view, either through the manager or directly to us.'

In order to contribute to the standard-setting process, users need:

— information about what a service should be providing and the quality standards which apply to it;

— the opportunity to take part in developing services;

— help in believing that they can express their real views, and in raising what may be their unreasonably low expectations.

Such involvement will not happen overnight. There will be disagreements, and some things will not be possible, perhaps because there is not enough money or staff, or because some needs simply cannot be met. The important thing is that all this is discussed openly, and that users, purchasers and providers co-operate in deciding what standards to aim for.

ADVISORY COMMITTEES

In all its work, the inspection unit will have the backup of an advisory committee, which should meet at least twice a year. The advisory committee will not have powers to make decisions, but it will advise and support the inspection unit. It should bring in the views of residential home providers and users of care or their representatives. Each local authority decides who should be on the advisory committee.

The Policy Guidance (Annex B to Chapter 5, para 2) made the following suggestions about who might be on an advisory committee:

■ a local authority residential care home manager (or managers);

■ proprietors of private residential homes, and representatives of voluntary organisations providing residential care;

■ private or voluntary providers of other services (for example, domiciliary care);

■ service users and carers;

■ representatives of the health authority or authorities with whom joint working arrangements are made;

■ a member or members of the social services committee;

- the Director of Social Services, or a member of SSD staff responsible for the inspection unit.

THE ROLE OF THE INSPECTION UNIT IN PLANNING AND CONTRACTING

The inspection unit will have an important part to play in developing the community care work of the social services department. In setting standards, it may contribute to the work of the contracting unit, which will be responsible for setting out the service or contract specifications which care home providers must meet. The inspection unit may also monitor the way the contract specifications are carried out. The advisory committee should be able to contribute the views of a wide variety of people and organisations to this process.

The public reports of the inspection unit should help local people learn more about the care which is available in their area. They should also inform the planning process, perhaps by showing where better training is required, or where more resources are needed.

Inspection units should help ensure that care for older people in residential homes is as good as possible. In some areas, where there is a strong tradition of inspection and resources are adequate to carry out the necessary tasks, this will certainly occur. But all the necessary work may not be carried out: the unit may face pressures from other work – for instance, in inspecting children's homes, and checking on childminders and nurseries, as prescribed by the Children Act 1989. Or there may be too many residential homes for the number of inspectors to cope with.

Some commentators have expressed doubts about the 'independence' of arms-length inspection units. They argue that the interests of users would be better protected by a fully independent inspectorate which could monitor residential *and* nursing homes, as well as other community care services. This proposal was not accepted by the Government in debate during the passage of the NHS and Community Care Act, although it proposes to review the situation in 1995. The role of inspection units will be just one of the many aspects of the community care changes which will need to be monitored and, if necessary, adapted and improved.

8 Paying for Care

In this chapter we look at the many different ways in which community care is paid for. First we discuss the charging arrangements for care in homes and care at home, before and after April 1993. It is necessary to understand these before looking at the transfer of public money from the Department of Social Security to social services authorities to help pay for the new arrangements. Then we look at some of the other sources of money which help to pay for community care.

THE TRANSFER OF FUNDS

The community care changes involve a major transfer of money from the Department of Social Security (DSS) to local authorities. As we saw in Chapter 2, the aim of this transfer is partly to limit the enormous growth in public spending on care in homes without adequate assessment of needs, and partly to make money available to provide more care in people's own homes. In order to understand what this transfer of money is expected to achieve, we need to look at the special income support system for residential and nursing home care, and at the changes which the post-1993 system will bring. This will affect how much money is available in the future to pay for care both in people's own homes and in care homes.

Paying for care in homes before April 1993

Until April 1993, people needing *residential* care could pay for it in three different ways. They could:

a   find and pay for a home themselves;

b   apply to the local authority for a place in one of their own 'Part III' homes, or a 'sponsored' place in an independent home – in both cases being assessed for their ability to pay the charges;

c   apply to the Department of Social Security (if their capital was no more than £8,000) for income support, which would bring their income up to certain national limits, depending on the type of care provided.

The situation was similar with *nursing home* care. People either found and paid for a place themselves; or were supported in a 'contractual place' by the health authority, which would pay the full cost of the place, as if the person were still a patient of the NHS; or turned to the income support system as above for help with the fees.

Paying for care in homes after April 1993

Special arrangements will apply to people who are already permanently resident in homes as at 31 March 1993. They will be covered by 'preserved' entitlement (described on pp 131–132) to the special rates of income support.

For new residents after 1 April 1993, local authorities will have the responsibility of arranging residential and nursing home care for which people need support from public funds over and above any social security benefits which they receive. (Some continuous nursing care will be the responsibility of health authorities – see pp 139–140.)

The options will now look somewhat different:

a   People who can afford to can find and pay for a home themselves, as before.

b   People who need residential care but who cannot afford it will have to approach the local authority for assessment to see whether the local authority will agree to place them in a home, and will then have their income and savings assessed to see how much they will pay themselves.

c   People who need continuing nursing care will come under either the local authority or the health authority – depending to some extent on local arrangements. If care is arranged by the health authority, no means test will be required; if the local authority arranges care, the assessment process will be the same as that in option **b**. The health authority must give approval to nursing home placements made by the local authority.

E

People paying for themselves can, as before April 1993, claim Attendance Allowance, or the care component of Disability Living Allowance. If their money subsequently runs low they may have to turn to the local authority for help, as described below. If financially supported by the local authority on a permanent basis, they will stop receiving Attendance Allowance or the care component of Disability Living Allowance after four weeks. The system will be slightly different for people in homes for a temporary stay.

Under option **b**, a national charging system will apply to people whom the local authority agrees to support in a care home. This new charging procedure will cover people in *all* homes where the local authority is arranging the place. The local authority will pay the cost of the place, and then collect as much as possible of that cost from the person being supported, plus any 'top-up' if the person has chosen a more expensive home. As with income support, the capital limit for help from the local authority is £8,000. If a person has more than £8,000 in savings, they will be expected to pay the full cost.

When supporting people with savings of £8,000 or less, the local authority will carry out a means test to see how much the person needs to pay, and how much the local authority's share (sometimes referred to as the 'care element') will be.

The local authority will encourage people to make up their income by claiming as much social security benefit as they are entitled to. This will include a new *residential allowance*, which will be paid as part of income support to people who qualify on financial grounds, in recognition of some of the housing costs of their care. This benefit will be paid at a uniform national rate (slightly more in London), but only to people in independent sector homes. The local authority will therefore have an incentive to make arrangements with independent sector homes, as residents in their own homes will not be eligible for residential allowance, and will therefore require a greater subsidy from the local authority towards their fees.

The local authority will then use the national charging rules to assess how much of a resident's income must be paid towards the fees, after allowing a certain sum for personal expenses. Most income, including state and occupational pensions, will be taken fully into account, although certain types of income are ignored, including the mobility component of Disability Living Allowance (which replaces Mobility Allowance).

This system will be similar to that which existed before April 1993 for people in homes run by the local authority (Part III homes), or who were supported by the local authority in independent sector homes. The system has been aligned with – but is not exactly the same as – the income support system.

In view of the new charging rules, all people already in Part III homes will be reassessed in April 1993 under the new system, which in most cases will be more generous than the existing Part III assessment. Where it is not, transitional arrangements will generally ensure that people are not immediately disadvantaged.

It should be noted that details of the charging procedure are complicated. Age Concern has detailed information in its factsheet series, which is regularly updated.

Under the income support system, people can 'top up' their fees if the income support and their own income are not enough to pay a home's fees. Topping up is possible under the new system if, for instance, a person wishes to live in a more expensive home than the local authority is willing to pay for. In such cases, the local authority will still be responsible for the fee. Either it will pay the provider, and collect from the resident their assessed contribution, plus the 'top-up'; or the resident will pay their share, plus the 'top-up', direct to the home, with the local authority paying the difference to the provider. If the 'top-up' fails to be paid, the local authority has responsibility for paying the full fee; but it has no obligation to continue the arrangement in the long term.

'Preserved entitlement' to income support

Some people will not come under the new arrangements. People living permanently in private and voluntary homes as at 31 March 1993 will continue to be covered under the old system: they will be covered by 'preserved entitlement' to income support. This means that people who are already claiming income support will continue to do so, and people who are in homes but paying for themselves will be able to claim the special income support rates if their savings drop to £8,000.

We have already noted that sometimes income support is not enough to pay the care home's fees. Where people have to 'top up' the income support from their own savings, it is possible to run out of money altogether, and no further support will be available from the DSS. Such people will have to look to charities or relatives – if they have them – for support. But charities may not be able to go on topping up for people in independent homes, or running their own homes at a loss. Private sector proprietors may also be unable to continue to provide care at the income support levels in some areas of the country.

Section 43 of the NHS and Community Care Act says that local authorities should *not* make arrangements for people who were in homes before 1 April 1993, except for groups specifically defined by the Secretary of State. These include people who may be evicted, for instance because a home is closing, or they cannot pay the fees and cannot find another home which they can afford. For people who have continuing nursing needs, it is possible that the health authority will have to make arrangements for them, if essential care cannot be paid for.

Paying for care in people's own homes

All this has been about paying for care in care homes. But a major aim of the community care changes is to make more money available to improve care in people's own homes. The charging system for day and domiciliary services will remain largely the same after April 1993 as before. At the time of writing the Department of Health planned to publish new guidance on this.

Each local authority will set its own charges, which means that different factors will be taken into account in assessing people's ability to pay. Some authorities may treat the Attendance Allowance or the care component of Disability Living Allowance as part of income, while other authorities may ignore it.

Although local authorities have the power to make charges, the charges must be 'reasonable'. A 1983 Act says that if a person 'satisfies' the authority providing the service that his or her means are insufficient, 'the authority shall not require him to pay more than it appears it is reasonably practical for him to pay'.[16]

Government Policy Guidance on assessment reinforces this statement by saying that local authorities should make arrangements

> so that users of services of all types pay what they can reasonably afford towards their costs. But the provision of services, whether or not the local authority is under a statutory duty to make provision, should not be related to the ability of the user or their families to meet the costs ... the assessment of financial means should, therefore, follow the assessment of need and decisions about service provision.   para 3.31

In trying to raise as much money as possible to pay for services, authorities have to face the dilemma that charges may stop some people from applying for help; but if they do not charge, they may not be able to provide as much help as they would like.

THE NEW FUNDING ARRANGEMENTS

Something over £2 billion was spent on residential and nursing home care in 1991–92 through the income support system. The transfer of some of this money to local authorities has been the subject of debate – about the amount of money to be transferred; about how it will be distributed among the local authorities; and about how much will be left behind with the Department of Social Security for their ongoing expenses.

The amount of the transfer

The money given each year to local authorities under the transfer system represents the 'best guess' as to how much the DSS *would* have spent under the old system on care in homes, less the money the DSS will still have to spend on people in homes, including the new residential allowance and ordinary income support.

Other money will be fed into the transfer as well – to take into account the number of people in homes who are expected to die or no longer to need the special income support rates during the year 1993–94, and for Attendance Allowance or the care component of Disability Living Allowance not paid, as referred to on page 130.

The DSS will retain the funds which it will continue to use for existing claimants receiving special income support rates, and for the estimated number of people currently paying for themselves who will run down their savings to £8,000, and then need to apply for special rates of income support under 'preserved entitlement'.

In 1993–94, the Government will transfer some £399 million to local authorities in England in respect of what would have been spent on income support (the 'transfer element'), plus an additional amount (£140 million) in respect of further costs related to their new responsibilities and the implementation of the final phase of the *Caring for People* reforms. This combined amount (£539 million) is called the Special Transitional Grant (STG). It will be 'ring-fenced' for spending on community care, and in the first year 85 per cent of the 'transfer element' must be spent on services independent of local authorities. In 1994–95 this money will be included in authorities' ordinary standard spending assessment baseline (see p 136), and an additional sum of £651 million will be transferred from DSS funds, again ring-fenced for community care. In 1995–96, the last year of the Special Transitional Grant, a transferred sum of £518 million is proposed. Again, this will be ring-fenced.

The Government has stated that after three years – from 1996 – money to pay for local authority responsibilities under the new system will no longer be ring-fenced. It will be calculated as part of the normal public expenditure process and will be paid to local authorities through the revenue support grant (see p 136).

Distribution of the transferred money

Local authorities want to be sure that the money transferred to them matches as closely as possible the numbers of people who may turn to them for help. The Government and the local authority associations have had long and complicated discussions to arrive at a formula for distributing the money which meets the needs of those involved.

The transferred money is replacing money which has been spent through income support on residential and nursing home care. But homes are spread very unevenly around the country. In some coastal areas, for instance, there are hundreds of homes, whereas in inner cities there may be only a few – sometimes none at all. Discussion has focused on whether the money should go to where the care is, or to the local authorities from which people have moved, to help them to build up services for people at home and in homes in their particular area.

In the first year of the transfer, 1993–94, the DSS transfer (£399 million) will be distributed as follows: half the money will be allocated according to the actual pattern of current income support spending for independent sector residential and nursing homes; and half will be based on the standard spending assessment formula. The £140 million additional sum will all be distributed according to the standard spending assessment formula.

In the following two years, the new transferred sums will be distributed according to former income support expenditure. But in each year an increasing amount will be distributed according to the standard spending assessment, as the previous year's grant becomes included in the baseline for calculating the new year's expenditure.

Will there be enough money?

One of the main concerns about the new system is whether there will be enough money for local authorities to carry out their new tasks – both to improve services for people living in their own homes and to support people in care homes. This anxiety arises partly from the fact that the special income support rates are not always high enough to pay for care in care homes. In some areas of the country there are few or no homes with fees at or below the income support national limits. People claiming income support and living in such homes have to turn to family or charities to top up the fees, as we have already seen. In some cases, homes prefer to keep residents rather than asking them to leave, even though residents cannot raise enough money to pay the fees.

All this has meant that there is a shortfall between the special rates of income support and the total cost of residential and nursing home care which it has supported. Local authorities have been worried that this shortfall will be transferred to them when they take on their new responsibilities. If the money being spent on income support was not enough to pay for the care already being provided, they doubt that it will be enough to pay for the care needed by new applicants for care after 1993, or for developing improved services for people in their own homes.

Whether this is true will depend in part on the local supply of care homes, and of other services which may help people to remain in their own homes. It will also depend on how much pressure there is on the local authority's budget.

Each local authority will be concerned that the amount of money transferred to it for its new duties should be enough for it to do the job properly. But the pattern of services in each authority will look very different, not only because of its unique population, but also because of what already exists there – health and housing provision, the transport system, and the kinds of services which it has had in the past.

These are all factors which the local authority associations such as the Association of Metropolitan Authorities and the Association of County Councils have discussed with the Government in order to make the transfer of funds work as well as possible. There has been disagreement about how much money is needed, and it will take time before we can see how the system is working in practice.

For the first three years, information will be published about how much money has gone to each authority from the transferred funds. Keeping track of what happens to the money will be an important way of checking on how the changes are working.

OTHER MONEY FOR COMMUNITY CARE

The focus of the community care changes has been on the transfer of funds. However, these transferred funds by no means represent all the money which is spent on community care.

Other local authority spending

Local authorities themselves have always spent considerable amounts on community care services. These include services such as home care and day care, as well as services such as sheltered housing, provided by local housing authorities. Local authority funds are raised in a variety of ways (see box on local authority finance).

WHERE LOCAL AUTHORITY MONEY COMES FROM

The revenue support grant and standard spending assessment

The largest part of a local authority's grant from central government comes through the revenue support grant: money raised from national taxation which is given to local authorities to run the services which they are required or enabled to provide by law.

The Government decides how much it thinks each local authority ought to have to spend to provide a standard level of services – this is called the 'standard spending assessment'. Such figures as the proportion of elderly people in the population are taken into account when calculating the standard spending assessment for an authority; but other important factors are not, such as the numbers of homeless people, or the number of elderly and disabled people from minority ethnic groups.

The local authority associations have said recently that the Government has underestimated the costs of providing services; they have expressed concern about the overall level of resources being made available for providing community care services.

Specific grants
The NHS and Community Care Act created two kinds of 'specific grant' – money which can only be spent on new services for people with a mental illness or people who misuse drugs or alcohol. Applications for the mental illness grant must first be agreed with health authorities, and local authorities must also contribute some of their own money to the cost of new projects. There is also a specific grant for training for community care.

The amount of money available for specific grants is relatively small, and there have been criticisms that new schemes have sometimes just propped up old services rather than introducing new ones. But the grants have also helped innovative new projects to be set up. They illustrate the use of 'ring-fenced' money.

Local taxation
Each local authority raises some funds through local taxation, formerly through rates, then through the Community Charge (Poll Tax), and from April 1993 through the Council Tax. In recent years the Government has put limits on the amounts which local authorities can raise in this way – this has been called 'capping'. Capping will also apply to the Council Tax.

Fees for services
Local authorities also raise money through fees which they can charge for certain services. For instance, they can charge for meals on wheels, home care or home help, and day care; but they cannot charge for social work services. Assessing people for their ability to pay for social services will be an important part of how community care works in any area, as we discussed on page 132.

Capital expenditure
If a local authority wishes to build new premises, or to undertake major renovations of buildings, it must apply to central government for permission to spend such money, up to certain limits set by the Government.

Community health care

Funds for hospital and community health care come from the budgets of health authorities, NHS Trusts and fundholding GPs. They cannot impose charges on individuals for NHS hospital and community health services (although dentists are able to make charges for their services). The availability of local hospital and community health care is thus outside the control of the local authority, yet is crucial to the authority's ability to arrange community care.

The Audit Commission, which monitors expenditure by local authorities, has now been given an additional responsibility of examining the 'economy, efficiency and effectiveness of health authorities' use of resources'. In order to improve community health services, the Audit Commission has recommended that ways be devised to 'pool' funds from different authorities, to ease the difficulties which can arise in providing services which affect different budgets. At the moment, it is difficult to mix money from social services and money from health authorities, except through a special process called joint finance, which has had limited success over the years.

Housing and housing services

Housing for rent is provided mainly by local authorities and housing associations. Both are funded partly by the Government. Government money for housing associations is allocated by the Housing Corporation, which was set up by the Government to fund and monitor the work of housing associations. Housing associations must also raise money from private financial institutions in order to build new properties.

Local authorities are actively discouraged from building new housing, with most of their finances going towards the maintenance and repair of their existing stock. They can also give grants to private owners (and in some cases to private tenants) whose homes are in need of repair, improvement or adaptation; some of this money is refunded by the Government.

The Government has cut expenditure on housing in recent years. In addition, local authorities were not permitted to reinvest all the money they made from selling council properties to tenants, although since November 1992 they have been allowed to spend any new money which they raised in this way.

Individual resources

Much of the money to pay for community care comes directly from the people who need such care and their carers. These funds include their own income and savings and social security benefits.

Some personal spending on community care represents 'hidden' costs. These include the sums of money which people do not earn because they have taken on caring tasks which mean that they have had to stop work, or work shorter hours. People who need care also spend money on the extra costs which disability or illness can bring – for heating, transport, special food, equipment and other such items – some of which are compensated for by social security benefits.

WHOSE RESPONSIBILITY?

We have already seen that although local authorities have the *lead* responsibility for community care they do not have the *sole* responsibility. For some people the greater part of their community care will be provided outside social services – perhaps by the housing authority or a housing association, or by the health authority. As already noted, there is potential for disputes to arise here.

Caring for People gives new responsibilities to local authorities to assess people for publicly supported places in nursing and residential homes. Yet it also states that health authorities retain responsibilities:

> There will . . . always be some people who cannot be supported in their own homes. Where such people require continuous care for reasons of ill-health, it will remain the responsibility of health authorities to provide for this . . . health authorities will need to ensure that their plans allow for the provision of continuous residential health care for those highly dependent people who need it.
>
> paras 4.20–21

The White Paper statement was rather overtaken by events in many health authorities, which have run down or completely ceased provision of long-term nursing care. In 1991 the Government said:

> Health authorities have a responsibility under the National Health Service Act to provide nursing care for those who cannot or do not wish to pay for it. Department of Health guidance is clear that people should not be discharged into private nursing homes when they have no wish to pay.[17]

This reinforces a similar statement in Department of Health Circular HC(89)5 which gives guidance to health authorities on hospital discharge procedures. The Circular sets out good practice which the Patient's Charter says should be followed by hospitals.

The Government has recognised the need for local and health authorities to sort out exactly who will take responsibility for continuing care in future, and has made agreement on procedures for purchase of continuous nursing care and for linking assessment and hospital discharge procedures a condition for receipt of the new Special Transitional Grant. However, there are no guidelines about what constitutes an 'adequate' supply of long-term care, nor about which people should be provided for within the National Health Service – for instance, those with a very high level of dependency, difficult behaviour or complicated care needs.

Bottom-line responsibilities

Under the special income support system for care home fees, people in homes can completely run out of money, as we have seen. The question arises as to whether there is a 'bottom line' below which a person cannot fall where one authority or another accepts responsibility for care.

A 68-year-old woman writing on behalf of her mother: 'I am writing to ask whether there would be any possibility of assistance with fees for my mother, who has lived in the above nursing home since October 1990, at which time the bed was fully funded by the Department of Social Security. This week the fees of the nursing home have increased to £315. DSS funding is £280, plus £12.20 personal expenses allowance. The shortfall is £22.80, leaving her nothing extra for her personal spending.

'I am a 68-year-old widow, and a pensioner, in receipt of housing benefit and a reduction in the Community Charge. There is absolutely no way in which I can meet the shortfall. My mother is 99 next birthday and I should like her to be happy for the remainder of her life.'

After April 1993, some 350,000 people will be covered under 'preserved entitlement' to income support. As we have seen, they may continue to face problems with a shortfall in fees.

Under the new system, the local authority will pay the full cost of a place which it arranges, and will assess residents for their ability to pay. There should be no question of a shortfall in fees for those who succeed in being supported.

However, a question mark remains about whether the amount of money made available to local authorities will be adequate to fund the necessary amount of continuing care; and about how health and local authorities will sort out responsibilities if demand for places is greater than either feels it can afford.

The 'bottom line' applies not only to people in care homes, but also to people in their own homes who need care and do not have sufficient resources to buy it. They will depend on the local authority to arrange appropriate social services under powers and duties set out in the laws described in Appendix 2; and on the health authority or a fundholding GP for appropriate hospital and community health services under provisions of the NHS Act 1977. Income support is paid as of right to people who qualify on financial grounds. The new system does not confer any 'rights' – or entitlement to care. Both local and health authorities have duties, under the National Assistance Act 1948 and the NHS Act 1977, to provide care, but these duties are not quantified. In the White Paper and elsewhere, the Government has stated that health and local authorities must work within the limits of 'available resources'.

People's access to support will depend on the policies of local and health authorities. For long-term nursing care, the new system for local authorities will lie alongside health authority responsibilities for providing continuous nursing care. For those assessed by the local authorities, formal means-testing is being introduced for health care arranged by them in nursing homes. How the balance will work between the centrally funded, free care available under the National Health Service, and the means-tested local authority care provided according to each authority's priorities, remains to be seen.

We saw in Chapter 6 (p 107) that where there is a problem, it will ultimately be up to the courts to decide to what extent statutory obligations must be met in respect of any particular person. In short, at the moment, we have no way of identifying where the 'bottom line' is.

9 Remembering the Person

In writing about the community care changes and attempting to understand their complexities, it is easy to forget what should be their central focus: the person needing support and his or her carer. Reflecting on the new provisions and procedures described in this book, we could well refer back to Annie, whose last years we briefly described in the Introduction.

We could think about whether an improved assessment system might have identified Annie's needs and led to more appropriate services being arranged for her. Perhaps the various workers who had contact with her could have worked in a more unified way. They could have asked her how she felt about the various services which were offered – why she rejected the meals service, how she felt about not having a home help, what she felt about her need for the security which the community alarm system might have offered. They might have tried to set up a service for Annie tailored to her specific needs, perhaps purchased from neighbours or local care agencies, rather than based solely within the existing statutory services.

On the other hand, she might have been assessed as not having high enough priority for the local authority to arrange services. In this case the changes would have made little difference to the way her story might have progressed.

Another way of thinking about Annie's experience of community care is to reflect on her needs and feelings as a *person*, rather than on the services which might or might not have been arranged for her. How might the ideals and the practice of the community care changes have affected the way her care was handled?

The Department of Health has described a set of 'core values' for community care:

a commitment to make sure that users and carers enjoy **rights of citizenship**, with equal access to service provision regardless of race, gender or disability;

respect for people's **independence** and their right to take risks;

regard for people's **privacy**;

understanding people's needs for **dignity** and **individuality**;

individual choice of services and how they are offered, within available resources;

service provision in a way which helps people **achieve their own goals** in everyday life. *Care Management and Assessment. Summary of Practice Guidance*, para 81

This statement of core values is very similar to the basic values relating to residential homes which we discussed in Chapter 7 (p 119). It forms a framework for reflecting on how the practice of the community care changes might relate to the ideals it describes.

The rights of citizenship

Annie was fortunate in that she could take part in decisions about her care; there was no obvious discrimination in her treatment. And yet she was very limited in her ability to participate. For her last year at home she was virtually housebound, dependent on others for transport to essential health services, and unable to walk out of doors. Her communication with the people offering services depended on their timetable, and on their willingness or ability to stop and talk.

The Government's core values state that there should be equal access to service provision regardless of disability, but this cannot happen if the disabled person is unable to participate meaningfully in making decisions about his or her care. Nor should the fact that people are old and disabled prevent constructive approaches to their problems.

The response to Mrs Akram's problems with the home care service initially reflected aspects of racism. Her ability to participate in the system and in her own care was strictly limited, because she could not communicate with the people providing her care. Developing an understanding of the needs of people in such situations may not always result in the solution of their problem, but it will recognise their rights as citizens to be understood and to have access to services on the basis of their need, not limited by the chance of their race, culture, sex or disability. This is a major theme of the Government's implementation guidance on the White Paper.

Respect for independence and the right to take risks

Independence is a difficult concept. Some people would argue that no one is truly independent: everyone depends on many other people. But in talking about community care we often talk about 'dependency', perhaps assuming that because a person needs help with, say, dressing, they are automatically dependent in other ways as well.

An important message of the changes is that care is about helping people with the care needs which they have, but not robbing them at the same time of their ability to take decisions about themselves, or to continue to do the things which they are able to do. This is where an emphasis on *services* can sometimes unwittingly undermine independence. One example is the provision of meals on wheels for someone who cannot get out to the shops. Providing transport to shops would preserve the person's freedom to choose what food to buy, even if they are dependent on someone to help them get there. Such an approach could have helped Annie to take a much more active part in her daily life.

Another aspect of independence is the difficult area of how much risk people should be allowed to take. In Chapter 4 (p 77) we saw that Mr O'Malley decided he would take the risk of remaining in his own home, rather than moving to a care home. Annie decided that she could not face the risk of falling again. Both were able to make their own decisions.

People whose decision-making capacity is adversely affected by illness or accident have decisions about their welfare made by others, to varying degrees. This can generate conflict between relatives, professionals and service users who have different views and it raises almost unanswerable questions about the basis for such decisions. At what point does a person's desire to remain in their own home become a matter of public concern? At what stage do professionals or families have the right to interfere with a person's independence?

As we saw in Chapter 4, these questions are closely linked with the development of assessment and care management systems. We have no legal basis for making decisions about care which override a person's autonomy. The Government's Guidance emphasises the need to give support to people who cannot make their own decisions. Advocacy is particularly important in this respect. However, the speed with which decisions sometimes have to be made; the agonies which face relatives, friends and carers as they watch a loved person's mental faculties decline; and the fear that something will happen for which others will be blamed, all contribute to the difficult reality that decisions are often taken in the belief that they are 'for the good' of the person concerned. There are certainly no easy answers here, but there is much room for reflection and further thought about how society copes with these complex issues.

Respect for privacy

Such questions are closely linked with notions of privacy. Support services have a way of intruding on privacy unless great care is taken. A contradiction arises between the belief in the importance of sharing information – between different professionals and workers, in the interests of co-operative working – and the need for confidentiality to protect the privacy of the service user.

In stressing the importance of confidentiality both in assessment and care management and in complaints procedures, the community care changes promote the idea of privacy. Yet there may be some contradictions. Where people have complex needs, information about their 'case' may be circulated much more widely than they realise.

Another way of looking at privacy is to think about people's ability to live privately – both in their own homes and in communal or group homes. It is often difficult for people with care needs to preserve their privacy if, for instance, care workers turn up at any time, with no prior warning. Carers and the person they care for may never be able to be alone; people in homes may have to share a room. Inspection units may increasingly check on how residents' privacy is being respected, yet the very idea of 'inspection' appears to contradict the idea of creating 'homelike' places for people to live.

Once again, great care is needed to make sure that systems devised for protecting people do their job well, yet do not intrude on the privacy of the people involved.

Respect for dignity and individuality

Respect for dignity and individuality arises from respect for the *person*. Some care needs – such as those arising from incontinence – threaten loss of dignity unless they are handled with sympathy and respect for the individual. Perhaps it is here that the *attitudes* of the service providers become paramount. If the idea is that positive steps need to be taken to minimise or eliminate the cause of the problem, then personal needs will be dealt with in a way which preserves the dignity of the person concerned. If, on the other hand, the idea is to 'get the job done', this will almost certainly be at the expense of the dignity of the person concerned.

A sense of loss of dignity may have been why Annie rejected meals on wheels. She felt demoralised as a person when the speed of delivery allowed no time for personal contact. Here, as with all the other aspects of community care and the changes, training plays a crucial role. It can help workers to develop positive attitudes towards others, respecting everyone's sense of worth; and it can teach them to carry out difficult or routine care tasks in ways which enhance rather than diminish the dignity of the person using the service.

In several parts of this book we have referred to the importance of training – both to implement the changes themselves and to improve the quality of care. The new National Vocational Qualifications (NVQs) have a major role to play in the working environment in helping care workers of all types to develop their capabilities. Training also has a role to play in bringing together people from different organisations and professions to share common themes of caring. It should also help discourage discriminatory attitudes.

Contracts will also be important in ensuring that dignity and individuality are respected. The White Paper and the Guidance stress the need to achieve value for money and cost effectiveness. It will be important that such aims include the need to obtain good quality services through respect for the dignity of the service user. Service specifications should make this clear in ways which can be checked on.

Individual choice of services and how they are offered

The idea of choice is central to the White Paper, yet we have seen that some of the new procedures may actually have the effect of limiting choice. Within the framework of the changes themselves, there may be more choice for some, and less or none at all for others. We have seen that the Government has placed a duty on local authorities to offer choice to people for whom they agree to arrange a place in residential and nursing homes.

The Government's 'core values' place 'choice' within the framework of 'available resources'. This raises the inevitable question of what are enough 'available resources' to allow what we think should be sufficient 'choice'. This issue will undoubtedly continue to be – as it has always been – the subject of much debate.

There are ways of offering choice, however, which do not require more resources to provide more or better services. They take us back to dignity, individuality and respect. They involve finding out how someone wishes to be addressed; offering genuine choice about when people eat meals or get out of bed; giving users a choice about who should be involved in providing their care. Too often all these choices are in the province of the *providers*, rather than the *users*..

All the community care changes should be ways of offering more choice to service users. Complaints procedures and inspection processes should actively aim to find out users' views, and to act on them; assessment and contracting should be carried out in line with users' views. How far these ideals will be possible in reality will depend partly on resources, but also on the attitudes of everyone involved. They will crucially involve providers learning how to work *with* rather than *for* users, in a genuine partnership of care.

Achieving their own goals

In order to achieve their own goals, people have to know what is possible. They need to know what their rights are; what might be achieved, given their particular condition or illness; what help *could* be available; and where to turn for advice or support. This involves providing information to people when they need it, and which they can understand and use.

It also involves service providers opening out to become 'enablers' rather than narrow providers of particular services or skills. The changes encourage multidisciplinary working – a difficult goal. But even good collaboration is not a goal in itself. It will only be successful if it succeeds in enabling service users to set their own goals and work towards achieving them.

This does not always mean more services. It may simply mean putting people in touch with information *about* their condition or problem, or creating groups of people to help themselves achieve their goals. Professional pride can sometimes cause suspicion of groups of people who may know more about coping with their particular problem than the professional. But if users are to achieve their own goals, they need to feel in control.

Listening is often the first step for providers in moving towards the goals of users. Some users may be very ambivalent about their goals, and need help in coming to terms with their changing needs. Annie could not reconcile her desire for independence with her growing fear of falling. Other users may not be able to express their own goals, and decisions may have to be taken on the basis of a judgement about what these might have been.

In Chapter 1, we compared community care to a jigsaw. Just some of the pieces of the puzzle have been described in this book. The White Paper and the Act aim to improve the fit of some of the pieces, but do not cover the whole puzzle. Even the pieces themselves have different characteristics: some are organisational, professional and financial; others are about attitudes, respect and abandoning stereotypes.

Bringing the puzzle together into one unified picture is probably an impossible goal, and may not be an appropriate aim. For *each person*, however, it is important to work as hard as possible to ensure that their community care jigsaw fits together as well as it possibly can. This means continuing to strive to make the practice of community care for each person match as closely as possible the ideals – an ongoing and never-ending challenge.

Glossary

This glossary explains some of the words and expressions most commonly used in talking about the community care changes. It is not a comprehensive list; many more words are explained in the text.

Assessment Part of the process of care management through which a person's needs are defined and a decision is made about what help can be arranged.

Care home Used in this book when referring to residential and nursing homes. Where discussing one or the other, this is made clear.

Care management A way of co-ordinating and arranging services for an individual person. There are different styles of care management.

Care manager A person who carries out the major tasks of care management. The care manager may control a budget, but is not generally involved in providing a particular service.

Carer A person who provides care and support for someone, but who is not employed to do so, and is not part of the 'formal' sector (local and health authorities, voluntary organisations and the private sector).

Caring for People The 1989 Government White Paper setting out what it proposed to do to change the funding and organisation of local authority social services for community care.

Community Wherever people live is part of the community, and is their home.

Community care Services and support to help anyone with care needs to live as independently as possible in their home.

Community care changes The changes introduced by the White Paper *Caring for People*, and (in England and Wales) by Part III of the NHS and Community Care Act 1990. (Part IV governs changes in Scotland.)

Community care plans Required annually of each local and health authority; to include information about the needs of the local population, and priorities and targets for meeting these.

Complaints procedure The process which every social services department must now have for listening and responding to comments and complaints from users (or potential users) of services.

Contracting The process through which local authorities will purchase services – either from providers in their own department, or from private or voluntary organisations.

Day care Different kinds of communal care almost always provided away from people's homes. Most commonly run by the local authority or voluntary organisations, with paid and/or unpaid workers.

Domiciliary care Services provided in people's own homes; includes home care, sitting services and bathing services. Most often provided by the local authority, but increasingly by private and voluntary organisations.

Griffiths Report *Community Care: Agenda for action*, by Sir Roy Griffiths, was published in 1988 and paved the way for the community care reforms.

Group home A house in which people have their own rooms, but communal facilities; staff may live in to offer support.

Independent sector Private, voluntary, charitable and not-for-profit organisations.

Inspection The process through which local authorities check on standards of care in all residential homes; and health authorities check on nursing homes.

Institutionalisation The negative effects institutions of all types have on residents and staff.

Learning disability Once described as 'mental handicap', or 'mental subnormality'. A permanent disability, usually occurring from birth, which affects learning abilities.

Nursing home Defined in the Registered Homes Act 1984 as 'any premises used, or intended to be used, for the reception of, and the provision of nursing for, persons suffering from any sickness, injury or infirmity'.

Policy Guidance As generally referred to in this book: *Caring for People in the Next Decade and Beyond*. Sets out what local authorities need to do to carry out the community care changes as defined in *Caring for People* and the NHS and Community Care Act 1990.

Practice Guidance Gives greater detail about how local authorities might implement different parts of the changes. For assessment and care management: *Managers' Guide, Practitioners' Guide*, and *Summary*. For purchasing and contracting: *Purchase of Service*. For complaints: *The Right to Complain*; for inspection: *Inspecting for Quality*. There is also Practice Guidance for training, including: *Training for Community Care. A joint approach*.

Purchaser–provider split The term used to describe the separation of two parts of one authority: one part assesses the needs of the local population and of individuals (the purchaser), and buys services from another part of the organisation (the provider).

Residential home A place providing board and personal care for people who need it because of 'old age, disablement, past or present dependence on alcohol or drugs or past or present mental disorder'. Homes for four or more people must be fully registered by the local authority. From April 1993 homes with one to three residents must be registered under a limited procedure.

Respite care Provides a break for a carer, either on a regular basis or occasionally. May be just a few hours or for one or more weeks. May be provided in a person's own home or in a residential or nursing home or hospital.

Ring-fencing Reserving money to be spent for a particular purpose.

Sheltered housing Specially designed housing with varying levels of support, available to rent from district councils or housing associations, or to buy privately.

Statutory sector Organisations created through Acts of Parliament – health authorities; local authorities; central government departments.

Targeting Identifying those in greatest need of service provision, and setting priorities to meet their needs.

Wagner Report A 1988 report of a committee led by Lady Wagner. *Residential Care: A positive choice* set out ways of improving care in homes.

Working for Patients The 1989 Government White Paper describing proposed changes in the organisation and management of the National Health Service.

References

[1] *The Prevalence of Disability among Adults* (1988), Jean Martin, Howard Meltzer and David Elliott (OPCS Surveys of Disability in Great Britain, Report 1), HMSO, London.

[2] *Housing: The foundation of community care* (1989), Alison Wertheimer, NFHA/MIND, London, 2nd edition.

[3] *Informal Carers: A study carried out on behalf of the Department of Health and Social Security as part of the 1985 Central Household Survey* (1988), Hazel Green, HMSO, London.

[4] *An Ageing Population* (1991), Fact Sheet 2, Family Policy Studies Centre, London.

[5] *Report of the Committee on Local Authority and Allied Personal Social Services* (1968), Cm 3703, HMSO, London, para 32.

[6] *Social Trends 19* (1989), HMSO, London.

[7] Letter from Andrew Foster and Herbert Laming to health and social services authorities and trusts: EL(92)65; CI(92)30, September 1992.

[8] *Community Care Plan 1992–93*, London Borough of Hammersmith.

[9] *Implementing Community Care. Improving independent sector involvement in community care planning* (1992) Department of Health, London.

[10] *Caring for People in Leicestershire. The Community Care Illustrative Plan 1991–92. Summary*, Leicestershire County Council Social Services Department.

[11] Mr David Mellor, 27 July 1989, Hansard, col W913.

[12] *Old and Clean* (1991), Age Concern Greater London, p 1.

[13] *Care in the Community. Definitions of health and social care. Developing an approach. A West Midlands study* (1991), National Association of Health Authorities and Trusts, Birmingham, p 14.

[14] Speech by Virginia Bottomley to Association of Directors of Social Services, 2 October 1992.

[15] Based on Section 2, 'Setting Standards', from the Department of Health/Social Services Inspectorate Caring for Quality publication, *Guidance on Standards for Residential Homes for Elderly People* (1990), HMSO, London.

[16] Health and Social Services and Social Security Adjudications Act 1983, section 17(1), (2) and (3).

[17] Department of Social Security and Department of Health: Memorandum to the House of Commons Social Security Select Committee, para 3.8, in *The Private Financing of Residential and Nursing Home Fees*. Minutes of Evidence. Tuesday 11 June 1991. House of Commons Social Security Committee. Session 1990–91. HC 421–iii. HMSO, London.

Appendix 1

The Disabled Persons (Services, Consultation and Representation) Act 1986*

Section 1 (not implemented): Appointment of authorised representatives of disabled people

An 'authorised representative' is defined as someone appointed by or on behalf of a disabled person to act as such for the purposes of the Act. A local authority may appoint a representative for a disabled person who appears to them to be unable to represent themselves by reason of any physical or mental incapacity. The DHSS (as it then was) is given regulation-making powers for local authorities to do this.

Section 2 (not implemented): Rights of authorised representatives of disabled people

This section requires the local authority to permit an authorised representative to act (at the request of the disabled person) as their representative in connection with the provision by the authority of any social services and also to accompany the disabled person to any meeting or interview in connection with the provision of such services. The authorised representative has a right of access to the disabled person at all reasonable times when they are living in a wide range of hospital or residential accommodation, including private residential homes and nursing homes. Initial arrangements are for representation in respect of social services, but the Act also allows these provisions to be extended to services provided by health authorities and to other services provided by local authorities.

---

* This summary is based on an undated summary of the Act by ACT NOW, the Campaign to Implement the Disabled Persons Act 1986, c/o RADAR, 25 Mortimer Street, London W1N 8AB.

Section 3 (not implemented): Assessment by local authorities of the needs of disabled people

This section requires local authorities (before they assess the needs of a disabled person for any social services provision) to allow the disabled person or their authorised representative to make representations as to their needs. If requested by the disabled person or the authorised representative, the authority must provide a written statement of its decision, specifying the needs accepted by the authority and the services it proposes to provide to meet them; or that in its opinion the disabled person has no needs; and the reasons for its decision.

If the local authority does not propose to provide a service to meet an identified need, it must also state this and explain the reasons why. There is a right to have the decision reviewed.

Section 4 (in force): Services under section 2 of the Chronically Sick and Disabled Persons (CSDP) Act 1970: the duty to consider the needs of disabled persons

The local authority must consider the needs of a disabled person for services under section 2 of the CSDP Act, if asked to do so by the disabled person or their authorised representative or carer. (This duty is *extended* under the NHS and Community Care Act: if a person is deemed to be disabled, assessment must be made *without* the person asking.)

Section 5 (in force): Assessment of disabled people leaving special education and Section 6 (in force): Review of expected leaving dates from full-time education of disabled people

(These sections are not within the scope of this book and are not described here.)

Section 7 (not implemented): Hospital discharge of people with mental disorder

This section sets out procedures to be followed at and before discharge of people treated for six months or more for 'mental disorder'. The Government has said it will not implement this section of the Act, as provisions of the NHS and Community Care Act will be an improvement on it.

Section 8 (in force): Duty of local authority to take into account abilities of carers

This section requires the local authority to take into account the ability of a carer to continue to provide care on a regular basis when assessing the needs of a disabled person living at home. Carers are defined as those who are providing a 'substantial amount of care'.

Section 9 (in force): Information

Social services departments are required to inform disabled people receiving any service from them of relevant services provided by the local authority or by any other authority or organisation, of which details are in the authority's possession. (This extends the CSDP Act, which refers only to other local authority social services.)

Section 10 (in force): Co-option to local authority committees of persons representing the interests of disabled people

Appropriate organisations of disabled people must be consulted before an appointment is made to a body or committee of someone with special knowledge of the needs of disabled people.

Section 11 (not implemented): Reports to Parliament

This section requires the Secretary of State to lay an annual report before Parliament on the development of community services for mentally ill and mentally handicapped people, the number of people receiving inpatient treatment for mental illness or mental handicap, analysed by age and length of stay, and other information.

Appendix 2

Acts of Parliament under which community care services are defined for the purposes of the NHS and Community Care Act

Community care services as defined in the NHS and Community Care Act 1990 are those provided under four Acts of Parliament.

National Assistance Act 1948

Part III: section 21(1), as amended by the NHS and Community Care Act, states that:

> It shall be the duty of every local authority . . . to provide:
>
> (a) residential accommodation for persons who, by reason of age, illness, disability or any other circumstances are in need of care and attention which is not otherwise available to them;
>
> (b) temporary accommodation for persons who are in urgent need thereof.

Local authorities 'shall have regard to the welfare of all persons for whom accommodation is being provided, and in particular to the need for providing accommodation of different descriptions'.

Section 47 of the Act provides for the compulsory removal from home to hospital or other suitable place of people for whom it is necessary to secure care and attention. These are people who

— are suffering from grave chronic disease or, being aged, infirm or physically incapacitated, are living in insanitary conditions, and

— are unable to devote to themselves and are not receiving from other persons, proper care and attention.

Section 47 describes the procedure for this.

Health Services and Public Health Act 1968

Section 45(1) of this Act gives local authorities *powers*, with the approval of the Secretary of State, to make arrangements to promote the welfare of old people:

> An authority may, with the approval of the Secretary of State, and, to such an extent as he may direct shall, make arrangements for promotion of the welfare of old people.

(In fact, the Secretary of State has never made such a direction, so this remains a *power* for the local authority, not a duty.)

Circular 19/71 described possible services to be provided under the Act, which could include:

— provision of meals and recreation;

— facilities or assistance in travelling to services;

— help in finding suitable households for boarding elderly persons;

— provision of visiting and advisory services and social work support;

— provision of practical assistance in the home, including assistance in the carrying out of works of adaptation or the provision of any additional facilities designed to secure greater safety, comfort or convenience;

— provision of wardens or contribution to the work of employing wardens on welfare functions in warden-assisted housing schemes;

— provision of warden services for occupiers of private housing.

National Health Service Act 1977

Schedule 8, para 3(1) states:

> It is the duty of every local social services authority to provide on such a scale as is adequate for the needs of their area, or to arrange for the provision on such a scale as is so adequate, of home help for households where help is required owing to the presence of –
>
> (a) a person who is suffering from illness, lying-in, an expectant mother, aged, handicapped as a result of having suffered from illness or by congenital deformity . . .

Local authorities are also given *powers* in Schedule 8, section 2(1)(a) and (b), to provide other possible services for people who are physically or mentally ill, including: day centres, meals, and social work support. Powers were also created for the provision of laundry services in households where home help is, or can be, provided.

These services are included in the definition of community care services by the 1990 Act.

Mental Health Act 1983

Section 117 of this Act imposes a duty on the District Health Authority and the social services department to provide aftercare services for certain patients, in co-operation with relevant voluntary agencies. Such services must be included in the community care plan of the local authority.

This duty is described in the Circulars on the care programme approach (HC(90)23/LASSL(90)11) (see p 78).

Further information

USEFUL ADDRESSES

Carers National Association
29 Chilworth Mews
London W2 3RG
Tel: 071-724 7776

Counsel and Care
Twyman House
16 Bonny Street
London NW1 9PG
Tel: 071-284 2541

The Relatives Association
(address as for Counsel and Care)
Tel: 071-284 2541

Local Government Ombudsman
21 Queen Anne's Gate
London SW1H 9BU
Tel: 071-222 5622

United Kingdom Home Care Association
Premier House
Holmes Road
Sowerby Bridge
West Yorkshire HX6 3LD
Tel: 0422 832559

RECOMMENDED READING

General

Basic Principles for working with older people who need care. A leaflet. Single copies free on receipt of sae, bulk copies £5 per 100. Available from Distribution Services, Age Concern England, Astral House, 1268 London Road, London SW16 4ER.

Caring for People. Community care in the next decade and beyond (1989) Cm 849, HMSO, London (White Paper).

Community Care: Agenda for action. A report to the Secretary of State for Social Services (1989) HMSO, London (Griffiths Report).

Community Care in the Next Decade and Beyond. Policy Guidance (1990) HMSO, London.

Community Life: A code of practice for community care (1990) Centre for Policy on Ageing, London.

Making a Reality of Community Care (1986) Audit Commission, HMSO, London.

National Health Service and Community Care Act 1990. HMSO, London. (Part III of this Act is about community care in England and Wales. Part IV is about community care in Scotland.)

Policy Guidance (as referred to in this book, see *Community Care in the Next Decade and Beyond*, above).

Report of a Study on Community Care (1981) Department of Health and Social Security, London.

Training for Community Care. A joint approach (1991) Department of Health Social Services Inspectorate, HMSO, London.

Community care plans

Circular LAC(91)16 *Secretary of State's Direction – Section 46 of the NHS and Community Care Act 1990: Community care plans* (September 1991). Available from DH Store, Health Publications Unit, No 2 Site, Manchester Road, Heywood, Lancs OL10 2PZ.

Housing and Community Care (1992) Circular 10/92 (Department of the Environment)/LAC(92)12 (Department of Health), HMSO, London.

Implementing Community Care. Improving independent sector involvement in community care planning (1992) KPMG Management Consulting/Department of Health, London.

Taking Part in Community Care Planning. The involvement of user groups, carer groups and voluntary groups (1991) Averil Osborn, Age Concern Scotland and the Nuffield Institute for Health Service Studies. Available from Age Concern Scotland, 54A Fountainbridge, Edinburgh EH3 9PT.

Working in Partnership. NCVO Codes of Guidance. No. 1: Community Care Plans (1991) Inter-Agency Service Team, National Council for Voluntary Organisations, Regents Wharf, 8 All Saints Street, London N1 9RL.

Care management and assessment

Care Management and Assessment. Managers' Guide (1991) Department of Health Social Services Inspectorate, Scottish Office Social Work Services Group, HMSO, London.

Care Management and Assessment. Practitioners' Guide (1991) Department of Health Social Services Inspectorate, Scottish Office Social Work Services Group, HMSO, London.

Care Management and Assessment. Summary of Practice Guidance (1991) Department of Health Social Services Inspectorate, Scottish Office Social Work Services Group, HMSO, London.

Getting the Message Across. A guide to developing and communicating policies, principles and procedures on assessment (1991) Department of Health Social Services Inspectorate, HMSO, London.

Purchasing and contracting

Purchase of Service. Practice Guidance and practice material for social services departments and other agencies (1991) Department of Health Social Services Inspectorate, HMSO, London.

Working in Partnership. NCVO Codes of Guidance. No. 2: Contracting (1991) National Council for Voluntary Organisations, Regents Wharf, 8 All Saints Street, London N1 9RL.

Complaints

The Right to Complain. Practice Guidance on complaints procedures in social services departments (1991) Department of Health Social Services Inspectorate, HMSO, London. (Included with this Practice Guidance document is a booklet: *Complaints about the Social Services Department. Ideas for a practice booklet for clerks, receptionists and telephonists.*)

Inspection units

Circular LAC(90)13 *Community Care Implementation: Inspection units* (November 1990). Available from DH Store, Health Publications Unit, No 2 Site, Manchester Road, Heywood, Lancs OL10 2PZ.

Inspecting for Quality. Guidance on practice for inspection units in social services departments and other agencies. Principles, issues and recommendations (1991) Department of Health Social Services Inspectorate, HMSO, London.

Inspection Units for Adults: Training implications (1991) Department of Health Social Services Inspectorate, HMSO, London.

Standards of Registration for Domiciliary Care (1992) Joint Advisory Group of Domiciliary Care Associations, Milton Keynes.

Standards and quality

Guidance on Standards for Residential Homes for Elderly People (1990) Department of Health Social Services Inspectorate, HMSO, London.

Guide to Standards in Day Care (1992) Age Concern England, London.·

Home Life. A code of practice for residential care. Report of a working party sponsored by the Department of Health and Social Security and convened by the Centre for Policy on Ageing under the Chairmanship of Kina, Lady Avebury (1984) Centre for Policy on Ageing, London.

Homes are for Living In (1989) Department of Health Social Services Inspectorate, HMSO, London.

Quality and Contracts in the Personal Social Services (1991) Association of Metropolitan Authorities, 35 Great Smith Street, London SW1P 3BJ.

Seeking users' views

Focus on Carers. A practical guide to planning and delivering community care services (1991) Janice Robinson and Lydie Yee, King's Fund Centre, London.

From Paternalism to Participation: Involving people in social services (1990) Suzy Croft and Peter Beresford, Open Services Project, Joseph Rowntree Foundation, York.

Power to the People. The key to responsive services in health and social care (1990) Liz Winn (ed), King's Fund Centre, London.

Putting People First. Consumer consultation and community care (1990) Discussion paper, Welsh Consumer Council, Castle Buildings, Womanby Street, Cardiff CF1 2BN.

User Involvement in Social Services. An annotated bibliography (1992) Tessa Harding and Angela Upton, National Institute for Social Work, London.

Institutionalisation

The Last Refuge (1962) Peter Townsend, Routledge and Kegan Paul, London.

Put Away: A sociological study of institutions for the mentally retarded (1969) Pauline Morris, Routledge and Kegan Paul, London.

Other useful reading

An Ageing Population (1991) Fact Sheet 2, Family Policy Studies Centre, London.

Care in the Community. Definitions of health and social care. Developing an approach. A West Midlands study (1991) Occasional NAHAT paper in conjunction with West Midlands RHA, Association of County Councils and Association of Metropolitan Authorities. National Association of Health Authorities and Trusts, Birmingham.

Community Care and Control (1992) Colin Fishwick, PEPAR Publications, Birmingham.

Decision Making and Mentally Incapacitated Adults (1991) Law Commission, London.

Home Help and Care: Rights, charging and reality (1992) Evelyn McEwen, Age Concern England, London.

Housing: The foundation of community care (1989) Alison Wertheimer, NFHA/MIND, London. 2nd edition.

Informal Carers: A study carried out on behalf of the Department of Health and Social Security as part of the 1985 General Household Survey (1988) Hazel Green, HMSO, London.

The Law and Vulnerable Elderly People (1986) ACE Books, London.

Multicultural Health Care and Rehabilitation of Older People (1991) Amanda Squires (ed), Edward Arnold and Age Concern, London.

Not such private places: a study of privacy and the lack of privacy for residents in private and voluntary residential and nursing homes in Greater London (1991) Counsel and Care, London.

Old and Clean (1991) Age Concern Greater London, London.

The Prevalence of Disability among Adults (1988) Jean Martin, Howard Meltzer and David Elliott (OPCS Surveys of Disability in Great Britain, Report 1) HMSO, London.

Race Relations Code of Practice in Primary Health Care Services for the elimination of racial discrimination and the promotion of equal opportunities (1992) Commission for Racial Equality, London.

Residential Care: A positive choice. Report of the independent review of residential care (1988) Chaired by Gillian Wagner, HMSO, London (Wagner Report).

Circular HC(90)24/LAC(90)10 *Specific Grant for the development of social care services for people with a mental illness* (1990). Available from DH Store, Health Publications Unit, No 2 Site, Manchester Road, Heywood, Lancs OL10 2PZ.

What if they hurt themselves: a discussion document on the uses and abuses of restraint in residential care and nursing homes for older people (1992) Counsel and Care, London.

Working for Patients (1989) Cm 555, HMSO, London (White Paper).

About Age Concern

The Community Care Handbook is one of a wide range of publications produced by Age Concern England – National Council on Ageing. In addition, Age Concern is actively engaged in training, information provision, research and campaigning for retired people and those who work with them. It is a registered charity dependent on public support for the continuation of its work.

Age Concern England links closely with Age Concern centres in Scotland, Wales and Northern Ireland to form a network of over 1,400 independent local UK groups. These groups, with the invaluable help of an estimated 250,000 volunteers, aim to improve the quality of life for older people and develop services appropriate to local needs and resources. These include advice and information, day care, visiting services, transport schemes, clubs, and specialist facilities for physically and mentally frail older people.

Age Concern England
1268 London Road
London SW16 4ER
Tel: 081-679 8000

Age Concern Wales
4th Floor
1 Cathedral Road
Cardiff CF1 9SD
Tel: 0222 371566

Age Concern Scotland
54A Fountainbridge
Edinburgh EH3 9PT
Tel: 031-228 5656

Age Concern Northern Ireland
3 Lower Crescent
Belfast BT7 1NR
Tel: 0232 245729

Publications from ◆C◆ Books

A wide range of titles is published by Age Concern England under the ACE Books imprint.

Health and Care

Taking Good Care: A handbook for care assistants
Jenyth Worsley

Written for all those concerned with caring for older people, this book covers such vital issues as communication skills, the medical and social problems encountered by carers, the role of the assistant, the resident's viewpoint and activities and group work.

£6.95   0–86242–072–5

Good Care Management: A guide to setting up and managing a residential home
Jenyth Worsley

This companion volume to *Taking Good Care* has been written for care home proprietors and managers, present and prospective. Topics covered include setting up a home, contracts, budgetary planning, staff management and training, the management of care and quality control.

£9.95   0–86242–104–7

A Warden's Guide to Healthcare in Sheltered Housing
Dr Anne Roberts

An invaluable guide for all wardens and care home proprietors on the health needs of older people and the best means of promoting better health for their residents.

£6.50   0–86242–052–0

Money Matters

Your Rights
Sally West

A highly acclaimed annual guide to the State benefits available to older people. Contains current information on Income Support, Housing Benefit and retirement pensions, among other matters, and provides advice on how to claim them.

Further information on application

Managing Other People's Money
Penny Letts

The management of money and property is usually a personal and private matter. However, there may come a time when someone else has to take over on either a temporary or a permanent basis. This book looks at the circumstances in which such a need could arise and provides a step-by-step guide to the arrangements which have to be made.

£5.95   0–86242–090–3

Policy

Age: The unrecognised discrimination
Edited by Evelyn McEwen

Comprising a series of discursive essays by leading specialists on evidence of age discrimination in British society today, including the fields of employment, healthcare, leisure and the voluntary sector, this book is an important contribution to the growing debate.

£9.95   0–86242–094–6

The Law and Vulnerable Elderly People
Edited by Sally Greengross

This report raises fundamental questions about the way society views and treats older people. The proposals put forward seek to enhance the self-determination and autonomy of vulnerable old people while ensuring that those who are physically or mentally frail are better protected in the future.

£6.50   0–86242–050–4

To order books, send a cheque or money order to the address below. Postage and packing are free. Credit card orders may be made on 081-679 8000.

ACE Books, Age Concern England, PO Box 9, London SW16 4EX.

SERVICE-RELATED BOOKLETS FROM AGE CONCERN

Community Care Changes
A series of five booklets on aspects of community care legislation and how to help your organisation thoroughly address these issues, £17.00 for the set or:

Complaints **£1.95**

Community Care Plans **£2.75**

Quality and Inspection **£5.00**

Purchasing and Contracting **£5.00**

Assessment and Care Management **£5.00**

Information is presented through a question and answer format.

Contracts and the Contract Culture
An introductory guide to assess the pros and cons of contracting for voluntary organisations and the questions you need to ask yourselves and the potential contractor. **£5.00**

Speak up for Yourself
Aims to provide a basic understanding of what advocacy means and to outline how the philosophy may be reflected in practice. **£2.00**

Standards in Day Care Services
Covers a range of services related to day care and how standards can be set and monitored. **£7.50**

Orders under £10 for service-related booklets should include a cheque payable to Age Concern England. Orders over £10 can be invoiced.

For further information or to order any of the above booklets, contact:

Fieldwork Services Unit
Age Concern England
1268 London Road
London SW16 4ER

Tel: 081-679 8000 ext 2304

INFORMATION FACTSHEETS

Age Concern England produces over 30 factsheets on a variety of subjects. Among these the following titles may be of interest to readers of this book:

Factsheet 6 *Finding Help at Home*

Factsheet 10 *Local Authority Charging Procedures for Residential and Nursing Home Care*

Factsheet 11 *Preserved Entitlement to Income Support for Residential and Nursing Homes*

Factsheet 29 *Finding Residential and Nursing Home Accommodation*

To order factsheets

Single copies are available free on receipt of a 9″ × 6″ sae. If you require a selection of factsheets or multiple copies totalling more than 10, charges will be given on request.

A complete set of factsheets is available in a ring binder at the current cost of £32, which includes the first year's subscription. The current cost for annual subscription for subsequent years is £12. There are different rates of subscription for people living abroad.

Factsheets are revised and updated throughout the year and membership of the subscription service will ensure that your information is always current.

For further information, or to order factsheets, write to:

Information and Policy Department
Age Concern England
1268 London Road
London SW16 4ER

Index